TOP SECRET/ TRADE SECRET

Accessing and
Safeguarding
Restricted Information

by Ellis Mount
and Wilda B. Newman

Neal-Schuman Publishers, Inc.
New York   London

Published by Neal-Schuman Publishers, Inc.
23 Cornelia Street
New York, NY 10014

Copyright © 1985 by Neal-Schuman Publishers, Inc.

Library of Congress Cataloging-in-Publication Data

Mount, Ellis.
    Top secret/trade secret.

    Includes index.
    1. Government information—United States.   2. Public
records—United States—Access control.   3. Defense
information, Classified—United States.   4. Business
records—United States.   5. Freedom of information—
United States.   I. Newman, Wilda B.   II. Title.
JK468.S4M65   1985   658.4'72   85-19864
ISBN 0-918212-90-1

Dedicated to our spouses,
Katherine and Edward,
and our respective children.

CONTENTS

State and Local Government
International and Foreign Information
Microfiche Copies of Documents

APPENDIXES

Preface

Over the years a sizable body of literature has developed which deals with the organization and retrieval of information. The emphasis has been on information which is readily available, either as published materials (books, journals, government documents for public sale) or items which can be obtained literally for the asking, such as manufacturers' brochures or free pamphlets.

The authors have observed that this large accumulation of literature, useful as it may be, has left relatively untouched the subject of the handling of restricted information, that which is safeguarded from access by unauthorized persons. These types of data fall into two main categories:

Military information of a classified nature.
Commercial information of a proprietary nature.

Recent events have made it clear that many organizations, including government agencies, have been lax in their efforts to safeguard restricted information. Both military and commercial data have been involved. Thus the authors of this book believe its publication is timely. It is obvious that more attention needs to be given to safeguarding sensitive information.

Another topic that has been infrequently discussed is the availability of certain government information which might seem out of reach for the average citizen unless he or she became aware of legal means of access provided for in recent years, a means of access that is all too frequently unknown by those seeking certain data.

Thus this book will deal with the safeguarding of military and commercial restricted information, along with the proper means of gaining access to it. The other major topic will be a review of laws that provide access to certain unclassified government information not generally thought to be available, together with a description of agencies likely to be sources of such data.

We feel this book would be useful in educational courses involving librarians, information center personnel and other information professionals. Still another group that would profit from this book is security managers, whose duties often include not only physical security for an organization but also protection of sensitive information, a responsibility far different from the usual security concern about locks, alarms, and impenetrable fences. Those responsible for records management are invariably concerned with the proper ways of handling restricted information.

The book is divided into five parts. Part 1 serves as an introduction to the nature of restricted information, the accessing of government information, and the relation of government data to information personnel.

Part 2 deals with military information, how it must be safeguarded and typical systems in existence for this purpose. Part 3 gives similar information for commercial information, how it can be safeguarded, and a description of how this is done in several types of businesses.

In Part 4 the role of computers is fully developed, with one chapter for military information and another for commercial data. Part 5 is devoted to sources of government information as well as methods of obtaining government information.

There are four appendixes which provide the full text of major legislation involving safeguarding and accessing government information.

We have not attempted here to deal in depth with certain topics, but we have tried to alert the reader to the problems, as well as specific tools and articles for use in pursuing in more detail certain topics, such as the government's increasing control of government-generated information. This is an issue of critical importance to our country. The involvement of information professionals in such basic issues is essential.

The authors have had many years of experience in libraries and information centers which dealt with restricted military and commercial information. This book is based in part on our practical experience. However, we did seek comments from other sources, and we would like to acknowledge the aid given by several people. First we thank Paula Strain, a very experienced librarian who was formerly employed at the MITRE Corporation before her recent retirement, for her time and attention given to reviewing the entire manuscript of this work. Next there are several people at organizations who provided us with valuable insights into their techniques of handling restricted information, some dealing with commercial data and some with military. For obvious reasons they have asked to remain anonymous, so we regret not being able to thank them by name for their invaluable help.

The authors would also like to express appreciation to the employees at the U.S. Department of Defense who, over many years, have been responsible for creating the indispensable reference tools, the *Industrial Security Manual* and the *Industrial Security Regulation*. These tools were heavily quoted in some chapters.

In addition a special note of thanks is extended by Wilda Newman to Robert R. Kepple, librarian, for many years, at The R.E. Gibson Library, Johns Hopkins University, Applied Physics Laboratory, for his special encouragement and support throughout her career. She is also indebted to the Catholic University of America and Dr. Raymond Vondran, Dean, School of Library and Information Science, for his support of her independent research as partial requirement for a Master of Science in Library Science—the results of which are included in this text. That work was performed under the very able guidance of her adviser Dr. Bahaa El-Hadidy.

It should also be noted that this manuscript was prepared using a personal computer and word processing software and then submitted to the publisher in electronic form, instead of the more traditional paper copy format. Edward Newman's technical expertise and assistance in this project was invaluable to its successful completion.

PART I
INTRODUCTION

We hold these truths to be self evident, that all men are created equal, that they are endowed by their Creator with certain unalienable Rights, that among these are Life, Liberty and the pursuit of Happiness. That to secure these rights, Governments are instituted among Men, deriving their just powers from the consent of the governed, That wherever any Form of Government becomes destructive of these ends, it is the Right of the People to alter or to abolish it, and to institute new Government, laying its foundation on such principles and organizing its powers in such form, as to them shall seem most likely to effect their Safety and Happiness.

Declaration of Independence, July 4, 1776

This part consists of two chapters of an introductory nature. Chapter 1 deals with several aspects of restricted information, including its basic nature, how it is safeguarded and the problems involved with it. It also covers gaining access to certain types of government information. Chapter 2 deals with government information in regard to its value, the role of the information professional in its handling, and the laws that govern access to this type of data.

Chapter One

Restricting and Accessing Information

Our society could well be said to run on information. We use information so much that we tend to take it for granted. We wake up to radio broadcasts of the latest news or the daily weather forecast. During the day we need data about many things—the price of goods we intend to purchase, the technical features of a service proposed for the business we run, the schedule of appointments for next week, and so on during working hours. We may have called colleagues for data, used a library, or had a search done on a computerized database. As we return home we might peruse reports and correspondence received during the day. Before the day comes to an end we have undoubtedly read at least one newspaper and perhaps checked the television guide to find out the schedule of programs. Our waking hours are filled with accessing and evaluating information.

Some information is simple to acquire. Other data may be difficult, if not impossible, to obtain. One reason for these difficulties may be the restrictions put on certain types of information by those who originate or safeguard it. Other information may be readily available to us, but perhaps we are ignorant about how to obtain it.

This chapter discusses two aspects of information handling. The first topic is how information can be safeguarded so as to prevent those not entitled to gain access to it from doing so. The second topic is legal access to information, particularly that which many people consider beyond reach, even if it is important for them to obtain it. Their ignorance of the proper channels may prevent them from taking the right steps in their quest for such data.

While these two aspects of information, controlling and accessing it, may seem to work at cross purposes, they are closely related to each other. Both topics are important to our society at this time, which has aptly been called the Age of Information.

HISTORY OF RESTRICTED INFORMATION

There have been restrictions placed on information since the earliest use of printed materials. An ancient document, going from one royal personage to another, would certainly have been intended only for the eyes of the notable to whom it was addressed. Precautions were taken to protect documents during delivery to prevent their falling into the hands of unauthorized people. It was essentially a crude system, relying upon weapons and brute force for avoidance of a security loss. As society became more complex over the centuries, there was an enlargement of the circle of those needing to control access to their records and correspondence. Safeguarding information gradually began to concern not only heads of governments and military leaders but also people in business, such as merchants, manufacturers, and inventors. The quantity of material to protect grew by leaps and bounds—chemical formulas devised by inventors, plans for military operations of armies and navies, trade secrets developed by manufacturing companies, sales campaign strategies to outsell competitors, and numerous other examples.

Due to the increase in the number of documents being treated on a restricted basis, methods of handling such data steadily became more complicated and formalized. Governments developed categories of restricted data, methods of marking documents became more regularized, and means of creation, distribution, and general control of classified documents were developed. Thousands of people became involved in safeguarding materials, whether in the role of a librarian or a security manager, or as a high-ranking official who would decide what should or should not be restricted.

Today we see a well-established set of procedures for controlling restricted information, both in business and in government. Elaborate methods are employed to safeguard print and nonprint materials throughout their life cycle, from the moment of their creation to their final state of being put into inactive storage, being destroyed, or being declassified after the need for secrecy has passed.

There is much at stake in having such security systems function smoothly and efficiently, while not impeding the normal flow of information any more than is necessary. The latter point is often overlooked by those responsible for the planning and operation of security systems.

WHY RESTRICT INFORMATION?

To many people the need to restrict access to certain information is obvious, but others may question the need for such limitations. There are two important areas of society in which restrictions are commonly imposed on access to certain data.

Military Security

It is unfortunately true, and probably obvious, that the world has not come close to the millennium when all countries will be at peace with one another. It is true that some nations have absolutely nothing to fear from each other; for example, there would be no need for a U.S. Department of Defense if the United States and Canada were the only two countries in the world. Since this is not the case, countries will continue to have military forces for defensive purposes. When military forces are needed, it is also prudent for a country to restrict access to certain important information, such as plans for new weapons, strengths of forces at certain key installations, or plans for the defense of the country, made up for future eventualities. This does not mean that implementation of a plan for restricting information would be a simple matter to handle or that it would be readily acceptable to all citizens of the country. Some of the problems are discussed in the next section.

Commercial Security

This country is founded on the principles of free enterprise, which call for open competition in the marketplace. This, too, seems to lead to an obvious conclusion that competing firms or enterprises could not really compete with each other if they freely shared their information on products, techniques, and business planning. What incentive would a research laboratory have in developing a new product, perhaps costing hundreds of thousands of dollars, if it were to share the fruits of the company's labors with a rival firm? Clearly there would be no point at all in trying to develop new products or devise creative marketing plans if one or more rivals were to be informed of details in advance. While patents provide a valuable measure of safety for the creation of new products or new processes, many bits of information vital to the success of a business venture cannot be patented; hence the need to keep certain internal information out of the hands of competitors. As in the case of military restrictions, commercial security methods may not find ready acceptance by all employees in a given organization, a topic mentioned in the next section.

There are other instances, of course, in which confidential treatment must be given certain information, such as personnel files, personal banking data, income tax data, personal and family matters, non-military operations of government units, and the like. While this type of data is not dealt with exhaustively, it is touched on throughout the text, as appropriate, and specifically as it relates to the Privacy Act. One of the basic aims of this book is to consider the current problems and techniques involved in the handling of restricted military and commercial information.

PROBLEMS IN RESTRICTING INFORMATION

The previous section pointed out the need for restricting access to certain information but did not stress the problems involved in doing so. The purpose of this section is to discuss some of the difficulties encountered by those charged with the safeguarding and restricting of commercial or military information. Some points will be seen as rather predictable, while others may not be apparent to those unfamiliar with security matters.

Need for Outwitting Spies and Thieves

This problem is quite obvious to everyone, even if only because of the familiarity we all have with novels, movies, and television programs dealing with espionage and theft. Security officers are often portrayed as bumbling and ineffective, unable to defend data against clever spies and thieves. Occasionally the opposite picture is given, with extremely clever security officers able to thwart the most ingenious plots. The truth probably lies somewhere between these two extremes. Security officers and their colleagues could not possibly be as ineffective as sometimes portrayed, yet neither are they supermen and superwomen with unusual powers of observation and strength. Most security officers make good use of modern technology and are neither indifferent nor overconfident in their efforts.

It is all too obvious, however, that some spies are able to do a great deal of damage before being detected, and trusted employees have often been guilty of illegal access and disposal of restricted information. Both military and commercial data are affected. Newspaper accounts of these cases sometimes make it seem that successful theft of data is happening constantly. Most people will acknowledge that it would be impossible to give a one hundred percent guarantee that every bit of restricted information of high sensitivity can be safe from falling into the wrong hands. However, security efforts are probably good enough that most data have at least a high level of safety.

Literature having to do with making a workplace physically secure should be of interest to our readers. It is a subject on which many excellent texts have been prepared, so it would be redundant to attempt to cover such material in this book. A good example of a treatise on this subject is the text by Healy.[1] He discusses plant layouts, physical barriers, alarm systems, lighting, vaults, and locks. A section on the role of computers in security systems is also included.

The importance of computers in protection of property and information is becoming increasingly apparent. For example, Bequai concentrates on the new breed of criminal who uses computers to commit fraud, theft, and other white collar crimes.[2] Part IV of this book will deal with the role of computers in restricting access to information.

Lack of a Suitable Policy

Restricting access to information is a difficult enough process to accomplish even when a well-thought-out policy governs decisions about what should be restricted or who should be denied access. Without a good policy, it is inevitable that restrictions will be applied haphazardly, perhaps subject at times to mere whim on the part of those deciding matters. In the case of military security, it is necessary that there be a national policy, ideally, set forth by Congress rather than by administrative units. In the case of commercial security, there should be a companywide policy governing all units.

Other Problems

Because restrictions on access to information impede the work of those needing the data, the amount of material restricted should be kept to a minimum. The gains made by informed people could well result in important new developments which more than compensate for potential loss of ground to competitors. Many writers have characterized this process as one of balancing the advantages of greater progress versus possible gains by competitors. Obviously both extreme positions are to be avoided. When material is overclassified, people working with it tend to lose faith in the credibility of the system and may become indifferent to the need for secrecy.

Restricted information needs regular reviews if those responsible for restrictions are to keep the system abreast of the times. Data get outdated, and today's secret information is tomorrow's common knowledge. This is more difficult for military security systems in view of the vast number of projects which may be classified at any one time, a problem not nearly so vexing in a commercial organization having much smaller quantities of materials to review.

The greater the number of people having the authority to decide what to restrict, the more likely it is that a uniform policy will not be followed. Also, the more people having this authority, the more likely that some of them would lack the judgment and technical knowledge of what to restrict.

The problems associated with restricting information have been the subject of many periodical articles, samples of which are reviewed here. An article by Harold C. Relyea, a specialist in American national government with the Congressional Research Service at the Library of Congress, is devoted to military security. He pays particular attention to the dangers to the scientific and technical sector of this country from what he feels are misguided efforts by the Reagan administration to limit access to commercial scientific and technical developments having implications for military operations. He cites examples in which he sees American scientific and technical progress being hampered by limitations on our scholars, scientists, and engineers. He stresses the need for rethinking federal policies towards restricting information of a non-classified nature.[3]

A broad study of the public and private aspects of the flow and availability of information in this country is found in an article by Robert M. Hayes, Dean of the Graduate School of Library and Information Science at the University of California at Los Angeles. He summarizes the findings of a recent task force established by the National Commission on Libraries and Information Science, one of whose recommendations was that Congress, rather than the executive department, be given the responsibility for determining what can and cannot be restricted in the name of "national security."[4]

Still another major issue is the position in which our universities find themselves regarding classified military information. In many schools one result of the campus unrest and riots of the 1960s was an upsurge of opposition to any involvement of universities with classified military research. In many schools a decision was made to ban any classified contracts being carried out on the campuses. While this may have denied the federal government the fruits of many excellent researchers, it may have enabled such people to pursue other projects which ultimately may bring more benefit to this country than involvement in development work on military hardware or applications.

At some universities the answer has been to establish separate units, away from the campus, which could carry on classified military research. A case in point is the Massachusetts Institute of Technology's Lincoln Laboratory, which has long held important classified military contracts. Units at the University of California have followed a similar plan. These developments illustrate the complications of restricted information in the academic world.

ELEMENTS OF RESTRICTED INFORMATION SYSTEMS

Whether one is handling information with a military classification or with commercial restrictions, there are certain basic elements of a system for handling such data which pertain to either type of material. The following factors illustrate aspects of systems for which decisions must be made in establishing a system for handling restricted information.

1. Scope of collection. What sort of materials will be included? For example, will there be only reports, or correspondence, or maps or audio recordings? How many items will be involved?

2. Degrees of sensitivity. How many categories will be required for the various levels of sensitivity? In commercial systems, what names will be given each category (already determined in typical military systems)? How will each category be defined as to contents?

3. Determination of restricted information. Who will have the authority to select materials to be marked as restricted and added to the collection?

4. Marking of material. What sort of markings will be used to identify the different levels of classification assigned to documents, correspondence, maps, and so forth?

5. Storage. In what sort of storage cabinets and in what type of an area will restricted items be stored? Will there be easy

access by those responsible for maintaining the collection? Will there be room for growth for a given number of years?

6. Indexing of information. What system will be used for indexing important features for each item so that it can be retrieved? Will retrieval be possible only by subject categories or will personal names, dates, originating organizational names, and other elements be included in the system?

7. Retrieval of information. What system will be used for locating requested items? Will there be a card file, a computer printed index, or an online system?

8. Loaning of items. What system will be used for loaning or distributing items to requesters? What sort of information will be needed to determine the eligibility of a requester to see a particular item? What sort of information about the recipient needs to be recorded, such as departmental unit, employee number, date received, due date (if any), description of item given out, and so on? How will audits of the records be performed?

9. Reclassification of items. Who will have the responsibility for either upgrading or downgrading the classification levels of items? How will all those in the organization learn of these changes? How will changes be marked, on the materials themselves or in the retrieval tools?

10. Weeding. How often will the collection be reviewed for possible items no longer needed? Who will have the responsibility for making final decisions? What changes will be needed for the records? Will there be any special problems in the disposal of the discarded materials?

Naturally, answers to these questions depend a great deal upon the particular system being developed. What works well in one case might be totally inadequate in another.

ACCESSING INFORMATION

One of the two major topics of this book is the matter of gaining access to information. However, the degree of accessibility varies greatly for different types of information. At one extreme is information that is so simple to access it hardly requires any effort at all, while at the other extreme is data that only a handful of people in the world know. Since most of us deal with a variety of access problems, it might be useful to describe major levels of difficulty.

Simple access. If you awoke one morning and had no idea what day it was, there would be many ways to find this out quickly, such as asking a member of the family or a roommate, looking at the calendar, checking a newspaper, or even calling a friend. This would be a trivial matter for someone living in modern society, although it might be a bit more difficult if one were alone in a forest. Another example would be using a simple reference tool (for example, a dictionary or general encyclopedia) to obtain an answer, such as a brief account of the climate of India or the spelling of an English word.

Moderately difficult access. Most of our access problems could be said to fall into this category. It is marked by a need for some sort of significant effort, whether we have to do some research or decide whom to ask for help or employ a special skill using informational tools to determine an answer. For example, to learn if a given Air Force contract has been awarded, we would need to know its number as well as likely people to call about it, assuming there is no one at hand to talk with. The more often such a problem occurs, the simpler it becomes. Even so, one hour after the decision for the contract was made, the answer would be quite difficult to find because so few people would know the status of the contract at that moment. As word spread through regular channels, it would then become more simple to ascertain. For instance, several government and commercial publications regularly carry this sort of data, with the delay in getting data published varying from one source to another. In each case, knowing whom to ask or what tool to use is essential to a quick solution.

Difficult access. This could include a variety of problems. One might be restrictions placed on certain data because of commercial or military security considerations. For example, the plans for a new submarine are hardly going to be available from the Navy for an inquirer unless he or she has a "need to know" and proper security credentials as well as employment with an organization which itself has the necessary security clearances. If these requirements are met, there is every likelihood that a person could, in time, obtain access to the plans. Thus this quest would be difficult but not impossible for those having the credentials named. Similarly it might be possible to learn the ingredients of a new chemical produced by Company X if one could satisfy its requirements for access. Again, some trade secrets are said to be so well-protected that rumors abound about how carefully certain commercial bits of data are guarded, such as access being limited to seven high-level employees in the firm who have never written the secret anywhere and who never travel on the same train or plane. In this case, access might be virtually impossible for a given employee of that firm.

What might seem to many people to be a major hurdle would be seeking access to certain unclassified data in government files. This information might appear, to the uninitiated, virtually impossible to obtain. For example, if a worker were injured on the job in a government laboratory, his or her access to records regarding the safety measures taken in that laboratory would seem like very difficult data to obtain. However, in recent years Congress has passed legislation that would make access to this sort of information quite feasible for people having a legitimate need for it.

One of the most significant laws is the Freedom of Information Act, which sets forth procedures for this process. More about this law will be found in later chapters. The important point about this sort of legislation is that access is provided to a whole range of so-called "gray" data, providing information which is unclassified but which is normally accessible only with the permission of those charged with keeping control of it. Both state and local documents are now commonly covered by similar laws, as well as federal data.

REFERENCES

1. Healy, Richard J. *Design for security.* 2d ed. New York: Wiley; 1983. 280p.

Written for those responsible for the physical security of a building, such as security managers, architects and construction engineers. Physical security is discussed in considerable detail, with many illustrations of equipment and their applications included.

2. Bequai, August. *How to prevent computer crime: a guide for managers.* New York: Wiley; 1983. 308p.

Discusses the various types of crimes that make use of computers, as well as ways in which such acts can be prevented or detected. A thorough treatment of the subject.

3. Relyea, Harold C. Shrouding the endless frontier—scientific communication and national security: considerations for a policy balance sheet. *Government Information Quarterly.* 1(1): 1–14; 1984 Feb.

Discusses the impact of federal efforts to tighten security in the areas of certain scientific and technical subjects, reflecting heightened concern by federal authorities over Iron Curtain competition for technological superiority. Effects on U.S. progress are discussed.

4. Hayes, Robert M. Politics and publishing in Washington: are our needs being met in the 80s? *Special Libraries.* 74(4): 322–331; 1983 Oct.

Discusses the growing concern over the trend toward broadening of the categories of data to be subject to security restrictions. Applicability of the First Amendment of the Constitution is also covered.

Chapter Two

Law and the
Information Professional

THE VALUE OF GOVERNMENT INFORMATION

Information provided by a government agency has certain characteristics that set it apart from data emanating from non-governmental sources. Much of what can be found in government publications is unique, because only a government agency could have access to certain raw data. Who but the Bureau of Census, for example, would have the basic figures from which the average income of families in Oklahoma or Brooklyn could be compiled? While it is true that even the federal government depends upon certain non-governmental sources for basic statistics, these generally involve only a few specific areas, such as the number of new cars sold each month or the number of new housing starts (this being a traditional measure of construction industry activity). The bulk of important statistics required by the business and financial sectors of our society is provided by government agencies. Having the power to subpoena witnesses is another example of how government agencies, such as a Senate or House investigating committee, can be the sole source of certain data.

Government publications are relatively free from commercial bias, unlike materials prepared by sources closely connected to the market place. For example, a Department of Commerce report would not be acceptable if it favored the interests of Company X over Company Y or Z. Any sign of bias would be quickly detected, and changes would be required. This impartiality can make a given bit of data from the government much more valuable than that prepared by a commercial source with financial interests in the outcome of a particular study.

Most government publications are either free or are priced below (or at least competitively with) commercial materials. Higher costs of some government publications in recent years, reflecting the viewpoints of a different administration, have reduced price differentials somewhat between the two types of materials, but the overall situation is basically unchanged.

Government publications cover almost every conceivable subject, whether in the physical sciences, the social sciences, or the humanities. There is literally something for everyone to be found in government publications.

Contrary to general opinions, government publications include far more than the traditional textual report. Both print and nonprint materials are included in these publications, ranging from video disks providing the latest technique for a surgeon to a detailed colored map showing topographic features in extraordinary detail. Handbooks, indexes to literature, computerized databases, color photographs or detailed tables of statistics are only a few of the formats in which government publications appear.

Some of the nation's outstanding scholars and leaders in certain disciplines are responsible for the preparation of many government publications. They and their agencies are often world-renowned authorities in their fields, lending an extra measure of value to reports and other informational materials originated by government sources.

It is only fair to acknowledge that not all government publications are outstandingly good. In fact political bias is one of the chief complaints about certain of these publications, bias not so much in the reporting of statistics and findings as in their interpretation. If bias appears in a government publication, it need not go unchallenged. Fortunately this country is blessed with a tradition of conscientious presentation of minority reports or dissenting opinion, helping to lessen the impact of differing political philosophies.

Librarians and information professionals have long concerned themselves with the accessibility of government information by the public. This concept was first put forth by our forefathers as an integral part of a democratic and informed public and is in fact protected by the United States Constitution, specifically, by the First Amendment, 1791:

> Congress shall make no law respecting an establishment of religion, or prohibiting the free exercise thereof; OR ABRIDGING THE FREEDOM OF SPEECH, OR OF THE PRESS; or the right

of the people peaceably to assemble, and to petition the Government for a redress of grievances.

Protection of the rights of the people from the federal government was expanded by the 14th Amendment to include protection from the state governments in 1865.

This concept reaches an even higher level of importance as our society, our culture and the world become increasingly complex and sophisticated. For example, James R. Ferguson looks at the First Amendment and dissemination of technological knowledge in his article, "Scientific Freedom, National Security, and the First Amendment."[1] There are new issues to consider, more laws governing our lives, and greater risks involved if our decisions are not based on facts, whether it be on a newly discovered drug treatment, an elected government official, or some aspect of nuclear research.

GOVERNMENT INFORMATION AND THE LAW

Laws Promoting Access[2]

Laws that promote access to government information while protecting the privacy of the individual include the Constitution of the United States of America and the Bill of Rights; Depository Library Program; Printing Act of 1895; Copyright Law (1909, Revised 1976); Freedom of Information Act (1966, Revised 1974); Federal Advisory Committee Act (1972); Privacy Act (1974); and the Sunshine Act (1976). In addition, state laws provide for access to state publications. A brief summary of these documents may be useful:

1. The Constitution of the United States was approved in 1789 and the Bill of Rights in 1796. These documents provide the basis of all our freedoms, not the least of which are "freedom of speech and freedom of the press," guaranteed by the First Amendment to the Constitution. The American press writes on all aspects of the government without censure or government interference.

2. The Depository Library Program, 1857 (which later became the Depository Library Act, 1962), provides for the systematic distribution of official government publications to the public through designated depository libraries. Such libraries must

maintain the collection permanently and provide the general public free access to such collections.

3. The Printing Act of 1895 had as its main objective to consolidate existing laws on the printing, binding, and distribution of public documents. It further requires that a comprehensive index of public documents be published, which evolved into the *Monthly Catalog of United States Government Publications*.

4. The Copyright Act, 1909 (now known under the title of General Revision of the Copyright Law, 1976) recognizes free access to official publications, none of which is copyrighted. Official publications have traditionally been considered to be public property and in the public domain.

5. The Freedom of Information Act, 1966, Revised 1974, allows access to official records and archival material as well as official publications which have been withheld from the public.

6. The Federal Advisory Committee Act, 1972, provides for open meetings of advisory committees of the executive branch, but permits closed meetings under nine exemptions.

7. The Privacy Act, 1974, allows an individual to determine what records pertaining to him or her have been collected, maintained, used, or disseminated by federal agencies and to gain access to those records.

8. The Sunshine Act, 1976, directs that federal agencies headed by a collegial body composed of two or more individual members be open to the public. This mostly includes independent regulatory commissions. Like the Federal Advisory Committee Act, it gives exemptions for closed meetings.

9. State Publications Depository Legislation provides for libraries to get state publications readily and automatically.

Part V of this book deals with the FOIA, the Privacy Act and the Sunshine Act in more depth. The state depository program is also addressed. The text of the three federal laws is included in the appendixes.

Laws Restricting or Limiting Access

There are several acts of legislation that are used to restrict or limit access to government information, both nationally and internationally, although in some cases that may not have been the original intent of the law. Several of these are noted here:

1. Espionage and Sabotage Acts and Conspiracy Statutes, as well as Executive Orders

2. National Security Act of 1947

3. Armed Services Procurement Act of 1947

4. Atomic Energy Act of 1954

5. National Aeronautics and Space Act of 1958

6. Federal Aviation Act of 1958

7. International Traffic in Arms Regulation (ITAR), Revised 1984

8. Export Control Act of 1949 and the Export Administration Act of 1969

9. Mutual Security Act of 1954, as amended

10. Inventions Secrecy Act of 1951, as amended

Part II of the text, Military Information, addresses these laws more specifically. Selected portions of the Espionage and Sabotage Acts and Conspiracy Statutes are included in the appendixes.

GOVERNMENT PUBLICATIONS AND THE INFORMATION PROFESSIONAL

Knowing the availability of government information and understanding the laws and rules of procedure for access to government publications is only part of the responsibility of information professionals. They have an equally important role in teaching their specific users.

Educating the Information Professional and the User

There are aspects, beyond simple acquisition of government information, to be dealt with by the managers of libraries or information centers. These questions could well be addressed by the manager of the organizations:

1. How do you determine what is available for acquisition?

2. What do you do in order to ensure that the acquired information is used?

Both aspects presume an educational role. The first educates the information professional relative to availability of government information, and the latter carries that knowledge through into reference work so as to ensure its actual use by the clientele.

Government controlled or generated data may include both security classified and unclassified information. Furthermore, information made available by the government or restricted by the government may change depending on several factors:

1. A change in the government administration for instance can change access to government information. Bruce W. Sanford, a leading First Amendment attorney in Washington, D.C., says, "The Reagan administration has dedicated itself to the proposition that the government that controls information best, governs best."[3]

2. Changes in some aspects of research and development in a specific field can change the government's role, for example in space research and development. Klaus P. Heiss[4] suggests that a United States open-market policy in space should be a cornerstone of United States policy. He believes that such a policy will bring about the most varied and dispersed uses of space applications and space sciences, while serving at the same time the best interests of the American people.

3. Perceived threats to the United States security has prompted Rep. George E. Brown, Jr. (D-Calif.) to speak on the floor of the House remarking that the Inventions Act, Executive Orders, and even the Freedom of Information Act are but a few ways this administration is restricting the flow of information.[5]

4. Perceived threats to the United States economy more recently caused the closing of meetings and withdrawing of scientific and technical papers, preventing information transfer to international conference participants.[6]

In the last few years we have seen another trend developing in the information arena: government information at a price, a price set by profit-making enterprises and most often not subsidized by government. This trend is seen by many as a threat to democracy and an informed public, by creating a class structure of information rich and information poor citizens.[7]

Activities of Professional Information Groups

Government's attitude toward information is usually monitored by societies for information professionals, elected officials, and the public. Following is a list of some professional organizations which indicates the breadth and scope of such activities.

1. The American Library Association (ALA), whose membership is over 35,000, has an office located in Washington, D.C., for the specific purpose of lobbying and alerting its members to the issues affecting their profession.

2. The ALA Government Documents Round Table (ALA/GODORT) studies specific issues related to government documents and publishes *Documents to the People* (DttP), a newsletter on developments in this field. It also specifies current activities and interests of the Round Table, publishes bibliographies, and lists new publications.

3. The Special Libraries Association (SLA) Committee on Government Information Services surveys the policies, services, and products of government information producing, publishing, and printing agencies. This effort is aimed specifically at how special librarians are affected and appropriate action is taken. SLA is an international organization of more than 11,000 members.

4. The National Commission on Libraries and Information Science (NCLIS) was established by Public Law 91-345 in 1970, as an independent agency of the executive branch, on recom-

mendation of the National Advisory Commission on Libraries. An example of their efforts is the study, published under Bernard M. Fry[8] in 1978, entitled *Government Publications, Their Role in the National Programs for Library and Information Services.* This looked at the current status of local, state, and federal levels of government publications. The specific questions it considered with respect to government documents included: Is there a need for a national center for government documents? What should be the relationship of the Government Printing Office (GPO) to the national program? How should state and local documents be made available nationally? What role should private enterprise play in publishing government information and in assuring its accessibility? How can government publications make a full contribution to the mainstream of useful and used information?

5. The Committee on Information Hangups, Washington, D.C., began in 1967 as an informal group concerned with "hangups" in acquiring government information. Its past efforts have included studies on the National Technical Information Service (NTIS), Defense Technical Information Center (DTIC), and the Government Printing Office (GPO). This work has prompted changes in government procedures, has promoted the use of government data, and has provided better service to the users of this body of information.

In recent years government information has taken on a greater importance. This can be attributed to the information explosion or the information revolution, compounded by the use of computer technology's allowing greater collection and manipulation of information. In addition, there is greater emphasis on information as a commodity and the resulting profits associated with such resources. One result of this is the challenge being made concerning the government's role in information. For example, the Information Industry Association (IIA) has been of paramount importance in the effort to move government out of the distribution and, in some cases, repackaging and distribution of government information.

Conducting Reference Work with Government Publications

Even though we have been discussing access to government publications, we should briefly address some of the problems recently identified that relate to the servicing and use of these publications in libraries.

The tenth study in librarianship, produced by ALA in 1983 under Charles R. McClure and Peter Hernon, *Improving the Quality of Reference Service for Government Publications*,[9] was based on exploratory research and, specifically, on how well depository library staff answered a prescribed set of test questions.

"The Depository Library Program is a cooperative venture in which the United States Government presently furnishes free publications to over 1,200 libraries throughout the country upon the commitment that they will maintain these collections for free access by the general public."[10] This program applies primarily to those publications printed by GPO. It should be kept in mind, however, that some of the publications available through NTIS and DTIC are also available through GPO and could be included in depository programs as "non-GPO" publications.

When studying the usage of official government publications, McClure and Hernon found that the general public will experience problems in gaining access to some depository collections and that documents staff members correctly answer a low percentage of test questions and infrequently engage in referral. Further, a library user has a better chance of receiving a correct response to a telephoned rather than an in-person request, and the length of the search process does not increase the likelihood of a correct answer. Two other points should be noted: (1) in a number of instances documents personnel admitted that they did not know the answer to the question but were unwilling to suggest referral, even to someone else on the library staff; and (2) the interpersonal communications skills of some documents personnel are limited, and these people can be abrasive in their dealings with the public.

While these results relate to the more "public" type of government information and reference services, it is not so far-fetched to extrapolate from these findings and suggest that the same or similar problems occur in the area of government information that is restricted or otherwise controlled by regulations and laws. It has been the authors' experience that the problems and challenges in this area are even greater, due in part to the fact that such information is not actively publicized or distributed because of its sensitive nature. Such information usually relates to military security and foreign affairs. It is essential, however, that the professional servicing the informational needs of an organization, whose requirements include this restricted area, know how to meet those needs effectively.

Bernard Fry addresses public documents and the depository program when he states:

> Library administrators need to consider government publications collections as an information resource on an equal basis with books and serials, to the extent that they are integrated in information services, whether shelved as separate collections as in many major research libraries. The relationship between the documents collection and other library collections should be that of a single resource in meeting user needs. To restate: the key to a good government documents collection is integration into the mainstream of library information services.[11]

The authors suggest the same approach to government restricted information, within the obvious handling requirements regarding security. However, the information professional needs more background and education in this area than he or she has previously had.

REFERENCES

1. Ferguson, James R. Scientific freedom, national security, and the First Amendment. *Science.* 221: 620–624; 1983 Aug. 12.

Discusses the Supreme Court's part in First Amendment law relative to dissemination of technical knowledge. It considers the Arms Export Control Act, the Export Administration Act of 1979, and the International Traffic in Arms Regulations.

2. Schwarzkopf, L. C. The Depository Library Program and access by the public to official publications of the United States Government. *Government Publications Review.* 5(2): 147–156; 1978.

Provides information on the programs for public access to government publications and information, a historical account, and issues and problems in the depository library system.

The authors are indebted to Schwarzkopf for his very thorough account of the depository library program and access to government publications, from which much of the information in this section was taken.

3. Sanford, Bruce W. The information-less age. *Special Libraries.* 74(4): 317–321; 1983 Oct.

This article was first presented as a speech at the SLA Annual Conference, June 1983. The author, a First Amendment Attorney in Washington, D.C., discusses the issue that our national allegiance to the idea that information has value is being challenged by current policies aimed at restricting what the American people learn about their government.

4. Heiss, Klaus P. Economic opportunities in space enterprise. *Journal of Contemporary Business.* 7(3): 63–80; 1978.

This discussion on the economic opportunities in space enterprise includes: (1) the development of global information systems; (2) large space structures applications; (3) space as an energy base for mankind; and (4) likely phases of space application development. The author sees the need for inspired national leadership, combining economic interest and technical and scientific enterprise as keys to an increased return on the investment made in space research.

5. Brown, George E., Jr. (Rep. D-Calif.) Restricting information-national security versus rights of citizens. *American Society for Information Science, Bulletin.* 8: 36–35; 1982 April.

Brown is chairman of the Subcommittee on Science, Research, and Technology of the House Committee on Science and Technology. This article was adapted from his remarks on the floor of the House, February 25, 1982. He indicates how some legislation is being used to withhold rather than disclose information.

6. Greenberg, Joel. Remote censoring: DOD blocks symposium papers. *Science News.* 122: 148–149; 1982 Sept. 4.

A news article that reports on the withdrawal of 100 scientific and technical papers from the 26th *Annual International Symposium of the Society of Photo-Optical Instrumentation Engineers* (SPIE), August 1982, by the Department of Defense and a "warning" telegram from the Department of Commerce. Thirty countries were in attendance including Soviet and Eastern European scientists.

7. Newman, Wilda B. Government publications: will an informed public be sacrificed in the name of private enterprise? *Science & Technology Libraries.* 3(2): 65–69; 1982 Winter.

An analysis is made of the future of the private sector in the handling of government information. Possible dangers to the general public that could result are discussed.

8. Fry, Bernard Mitchell, editor. *Government publications, their role in the National Program for Library and Information Services.* Washington: Na-

tional Commission on Libraries and Information Science; 1978 Dec.; GPO SNO 52 003 00648-1. 128p.

Addresses five questions, noted here in the text, and highlights the implications for change in the areas studied.

9. McClure, Charles R.; Hernon, Peter. *Improving the quality of reference service for government publications*. Chicago: American Libraries Association; 1983. 270p. (ALA Studies in Librarianship, No. 10).

Uses exploratory research methods to consider document reference service relative to general reference service. It gives an overview of strategies that can be used to better exploit government publications.

10. Schwarzkopf.

11. Fry, Bernard Mitchell. Government publications and the library: implications for change. *Government Publications Review*. 4(2): 111–117; 1977.

Looks at the problems in the acquisition and dissemination of government publications and suggests that this information resource be incorporated into the mainstream of library services.

PART II
MILITARY INFORMATION

Carelessness about our security is dangerous; carelessness about our freedom is also dangerous.

Adlai Stevenson, 1952

This part discusses military information. The first of the two chapters looks at the U.S. Government Security Program and its requirements for safeguarding military information. Chapter 4 describes the specifics used for handling military information.

Chapter Three

Requirements for Safeguarding Military Information

Many different systems are used in this country for safeguarding military information. All, however, are based on one specific type or model, the U.S. Security Program.[1] This program sets the rules, enforces the laws, monitors the facilities, and so forth. Within the program, government agencies set up their own systems for security, and government contractors have additional internal systems as well. For example, the Department of Defense—Army, Navy (including the Marines), and Air Force—all have separate systems. They issue their own regulations, directives, and procedures. These can be different from one another, but each must meet the specifications of the Security Program.

Rather than looking at each military department system we will deal with the U.S. Security Program. It is more important, for the moment, to show in some detail how the program is structured, what agencies are involved, and its laws and administration.

UNITED STATES LAW AND INDUSTRIAL SECURITY

The following list includes some of the government laws and directives used to restrict or limit access to government information, both nationally and internationally, although that may not have been the original intention of the legislation. Furthermore, on looking at the stated purpose of such laws it may appear that it is not at all related to the control of information. While some laws state their implications relative to "national security," others have been interpreted in a rather creative fashion in order to use them to control the flow of information.

Espionage and Sabotage Acts and Conspiracy Statutes. The espionage and sabotage acts, and the conspiracy statutes appear in the U.S. Code, Title 18, Crimes and Criminal Procedure. Chapter 19 is on conspiracy, Chapter 37 covers espionage and censorship, and Chapter 105 is on sabotage. Title 50, War and National Defense, Chapter 23 is on internal security. Sub-chapter I covers subversive activities. Excerpts are included in the appendixes.[2]

Internal Security Act, 1950. The main approach of this law was exposure—through complicated machinery requiring the registration of legally determined Communist-action and Communist-front organizations. In a later amendment any organization required by law to register as a Communist-action or front group had also to register all of its printing equipment.[3]

National Security Act of 1947 (became law in 1950). This Act was to provide a comprehensive program for the future security of the United States, and gave the three services authoritative coordination and unified direction under civilian control, but did not merge them. This Act also created the Central Intelligence Agency (CIA).[4]

Armed Services Procurement Act of 1947 (as amended). This Act specifies that it is in the interest of the United States to acquire property and services for the Department of Defense in the most timely, economic, and efficient manner possible. It establishes uniform policies and procedures relating to the procurement of supplies and services. The Act requires that competitive bids be used along with advertising; however, there are exceptions, e.g., where services or property should not be publicly disclosed because of their character, ingredients, or components.[5]

Atomic Energy Act, 1954. This Act was passed in recognition of the fact that atomic energy has applications for peaceful as well as military purposes. This Act provides for the development, use, and control of atomic energy so as to promote world peace, improve the general welfare, increase the standard of living, and strengthen free competition in private enterprise, while ensuring common defense and security in the United States.[6]

Executive Order 10104, February 1, 1950. This Order concerns vital military and naval installations and equipment requiring protection against the general dissemination of information.[7]

Executive Order 12356, April 6, 1982. This Order specifies the program for National Security Information in the United States. It details a uniform system for classifying, declassifying, and safeguarding national security information, signed by President Ronald Reagan.[8] It revoked Executive Order 12065.

National Aeronautics and Space Act of 1958. This declares that it is the policy of the United States ". . . that activities in space should be devoted to peaceful purposes for the benefit of all mankind." Under the law the President is responsible for developing a comprehensive program of space activities; it also assigned military applications to the Defense Department. Non-military programs were assigned to the National Aeronautics and Space Administration (NASA) and headed by a civilian administrator.[9]

Executive Order 10865, 1 February 20, 1960. This Order is on safeguarding government classified information within industry.[10]

Federal Aviation Act of 1958. It created the Federal Aviation Agency (FAA) which assumed authority over the nation's air space. The FAA Administrator regulates the use of navigable air space by military as well as civilian aircraft and provides for the establishment of restricted air space zones for security identification of aircraft.[11]

Executive Order 10909, January 17, 1961. This Order amends Executive Order 10865 on safeguarding classified information within industry.[12]

International Traffic in Arms Regulation (ITAR). This regulation covers arms, ammunition, and implements of war and the importation of arms, ammunition, and implements of war. It is published as part of the *Code of Federal Regulations.*[13]

Export Control Act of 1949 (became the Export Administration Act of 1969). It authorizes the President to prohibit or curtail the export of any articles, materials, or supplies to meet the requirements of goods at home and to maintain controls over exports to the Communist bloc.[14] This was replaced by the Export Administration Act of 1969 which set up a system under which licenses were required for shipment of certain items to Communist countries. The 1969 Act carried forth the provision that the President could prohibit all trade for reasons of national security.[15]

Mutual Security Act of 1954 (as amended). This provides for foreign aid, both economic and military.[16]

Executive Order 12065, June 28, 1978. This Order specified the program for National Security Information in the United States. Its aim was to balance the public interest in access to government information and at the same time protect certain national security information from disclosure.[17] This Order was signed by Jimmy Carter, as President in 1978. It was revoked by Executive Order 12356.[18]

Information Security Oversight Office (ISOO). The ISOO ensures compliance with Executive Order 12065, National Security Information. In doing so it hears appeals on declassification, develops binding directives on the agencies, reviews declassification programs in the agencies and may conduct on-site reviews of agency information security programs.[19] Executive Order 12356 continued the ISOO.

Inventions Secrecy Act of 1954 (as amended). This Act grants the right of a government agency to withhold the grant of a patent and the invention kept secret if in the opinion of the agency disclosure is detrimental to national security.[20]

Department of Defense Directive 5230.24. This Directive covers all newly created technical documents generated by DOD funded research, development, test and evaluation (RDT&E) programs, which are the basis of the DOD Scientific and Technical Information Program. This Directive specifies the Distribution Statements for such information whether it is classified or unclassified.[21]

THE UNITED STATES SECURITY PROGRAM

According to Thomas J. O'Brien, Director, Defense Investigative Service, the "... *Industrial Security Manual* is issued under the directional authority of, and in accordance with, Department of Defense (DOD) Directive 5220.22, Department of Defense Industrial Security Program. It establishes uniform security practices within industrial plants, educational institutions, and all organizations and facilities used by prime contractors and subcontractors having classified information of the Department of Defense, certain other executive departments and agencies, or certain foreign governments. . . . It is issued pursuant to and constitutes notice prescribed by Section

1A(i) of DD Form 441, Department of Defense Security Agreement, January 1984 and Section 1A of DIS Form 1149, Department of Defense Transportation Security Agreement, January 1981."[22]

Structure of U.S. Security Services

The industrial security services in the United States are under the Secretary of Defense and act on behalf of other government departments and agencies in such matters. These include the Office of Secretary of Defense and its boards, councils, staffs, and commands; DOD agencies; Departments of State, Commerce, Treasury, Transportation, Interior, Agriculture, Health and Human Services, Labor, and Justice; National Aeronautics and Space Administration; General Services Administration; Small Business Administration; National Science Foundation; Arms Control and Disarmament Agency; Federal Emergency Management Agency; General Accounting Office; and Federal Reserve System.

Overall policy guidance is provided by the Deputy Under Secretary of Defense for Policy.

Administration of Industrial Security

The Director, Defense Investigative Service (DIS) is responsible for the administration of the DOD Industrial Security Program on behalf of the user agencies, noted above.

The DIS has eight regional offices with specific boundaries. The regions are Northwestern, San Francisco, including Alaska; Pacific, Los Angeles, including Hawaii, U.S. possessions and Trust Territories; Southwestern, St. Louis; Mid-Western, Cleveland; Southeastern, Atlanta, including Puerto Rico, Panama Canal Zone, and U.S. possessions in the Atlantic and Caribbean; New England, Boston; Mid-Atlantic, Philadelphia; and Washington, D.C., Capital region, which includes Virginia, D.C., and part of Maryland. The Director of Industrial Security in each region is designated as the cognizant security office for all contractor facilities located within the region.

Support Activities

There are three support activities. These are the Defense Industrial Security Clearance Office (DISCO), Columbus, Ohio; the Defense Security Institute (DSI), Richmond, Virginia, (formerly the Defense Industrial Security Institute (DISI)); and the Office of Industrial Security, International (OISI), in Brussels, Belgium. Defense Industrial Security Clearance Office (DISCO) is responsible for personnel security clearances which grant access to individuals for classified information in specified categories. Defense Security Institute (DSI), established by the Deputy Secretary of Defense, is administered by the Defense Investigative Service. The Institute comprises four Departments, three engaged in classroom instruction and one in security education and extension production. The instructional departments include Industrial Security, Information Security, and Personnel Security Investigations. The Educational Programs Department includes the Security Awareness and Correspondence Course Divisions.

Office of Industrial Security Institute (OISI), established by DOD, provides administrative assistance for industrial security purposes to U.S. industry in their marketing, liaison, and technical assistance activities outside the U.S. It assists U.S. industry by: (1) arranging classified visits for U.S. contractor employees; (2) providing storage for classified material; (3) providing mail channels for classified material between a contractor in the U.S. and an approved destination outside the U.S., when specifically authorized by the Deputy Director (Industrial Security), Headquarters, Defense Investigative Service; (4) providing security briefings and security certificates, as appropriate; and (5) providing assistance on security matters, such as visits to military activities or contractors outside the U.S.

Classified Information Requirements

Generally, these three requirements must be met before classified information may be released:

1. There must be a "need to know" for that data based on work requirements for a government contract. The contracting agency has to certify the "need to know" in some official manner.

2. The potential user must have facilities for storage and distribution of classified information that have been cleared by a security agency as satisfactory for such use.

3. The persons who will handle or use the classified data must have been granted a security clearance of the appropriate level by the U.S. Government.

The *Industrial Security Manual* explains how these requirements may be met.

DOD and Other Forms for U.S. Security

An organization wishing to do business with the government under classified contracts is required to use a number of industrial security forms. Although the information professional working with such a contract may never make personal use of many of these forms, he or she should be aware of their existence. Seventeen are described below, with a brief description of the use and purpose of each. All are needed in order to comply with government security requirements, but some are prepared by the contractor and others by the government office with which the contractor works.

1. Department of Defense Personnel Questionnaire (Industrial-NAC) (DD Form 48)
    This form is used to obtain personal data from a U.S. citizen being considered for a DOD CONFIDENTIAL or SECRET personnel security clearance.

2. Application and Authorization for Access to Confidential Information (Industrial) (DD Form 48-2)
    This form serves the same purpose as the DD Form 48, listed above, but is for a CONFIDENTIAL personnel security clearance.

3. Department of Defense Personnel Security Questionnaire (Updating) (DD Form 48-3)
    This form is used to obtain current personal data when an individual with a security clearance is transferring employment from one contractor to another within a twelve-month period and still requires a clearance. It is also used in converting a user agency clearance to an industrial security clearance.

4. Department of Defense Personnel Security Questionnaire (Industrial) (DD Form 49)
    This form is used for a U.S. citizen being considered for a TOP SECRET personnel security clearance, for any level of clearance for an individual that is a representative of a foreign interest, individual that has relatives in a Communist country, that is an immigrant alien being considered for a clearance, and a citizen of a signatory country being processed for a reciprocal clearance.

5. Department of Defense Contract Security Classification Specification (DD Form 254)

This form, along with appropriate attachments, serves as the basic document by which classification, regrading, and declassification specifications are documented and provided to prime contractors and subcontractors. It identifies the specific items of classified information involved in the contract that require security.

6. Applicant Fingerprint Card (DD Form 258)

This form is completed for all personnel being considered by the Defense Industrial Security Clearance Office (DISCO) for a personnel security clearance.

7. Request for Visit or Access Approval (DOE F 5631.20)

This form, available from the Department of Energy (DOE), is used for processing visits involving access to RESTRICTED DATA.

8. Letter of Notification of Facility Security Clearance (DIS FL 381-R)

This letter is used by the Defense Investigative Service to notify a facility that it has been granted a facility security clearance.

9. Department of Defense Security Agreement (DD Form 441) and Appendage (DD Form 441-1)

This form is used to obtain the formal agreement of management of a facility to abide by the *DOD Industrial Security Manual for Safeguarding Classified Information*. The Appendage is used for coverage of multiple facilities, and for additions, deletions, or changes.

10. Certificate Pertaining to Foreign Interests (DD Form 441s)

This form is used to provide formal certification from the contractor of foreign ownership, control, or influence, in order that eligibility for a facility security clearance may be determined by DOD.

11. Security Briefing and Termination Statements (Industrial Personnel) (DISCO Form 482)

This two-part form is for use by employees of contractors. Part I is for employees, following their initial security briefings prior to being granted access to classified information, to certify that they have read and are familiar with the provisions of the espionage laws and other federal criminal statutes applicable to the safeguarding of classified information. Part II is used by employees during termination proceedings to make like declarations.

12. Letter of Consent (DISCO Form 560)

The DISCO letter of consent is used to notify a facility that an employee is authorized to have access to a specific category of classified information.

13. Personnel Security Clearance Change Notification (DISCO Form 562)

This multipurpose form is used by the contractor to report occurrences concerning a cleared employee or one being cleared. For example, termination, change of name, multiple facility transfer, collocated cleared facilities transfer, reinstatement of clearance, downgrading of a TOP SECRET clearance or reinstatement of a previously downgraded TOP SECRET clearance.

14. Department of Defense Transportation Security Agreement (DIS Form 1149)

This form is used by the cognizant security office in obtaining the formal agreement of the home office facility of the commercial carrier to abide by the *Industrial Security Manual for Safeguarding Classified Information.*

15. Facility Clearance Register (DD Form 1541)

This form provides for uniform certification of a facility's clearance and safeguarding ability to the Defense Technical Information Center (DTIC) and notifies DTIC of changes affecting an existing certification.

16. Registration for Scientific and Technical Information Services (DD Form 1540)

This form is used to establish eligibility for the information, reference, and distribution services of DTIC.

17. Letter Agreement to Safeguard Classified Information for an Employee Performing Consultant Services.

In completing this agreement a contractor accepts responsibility for safeguarding classified information released to an employee furnishing consultant services.

Complete instructions on how to fill out these forms, as well as samples, can be found in the *Industrial Security Manual for Safeguarding Classified Information.*

REFERENCES

1. U.S. Department of Defense. *Industrial security manual for safeguarding classified information*. Washington: GPO; 1984 Mar.; DOD 5220.22-M. 345p.

This tool, as noted in the text, establishes uniform security practices as determined by the U.S. Government.

2. *United States Code*. Title 18 and Title 50, 1982 edition. Washington: GPO; 1983.

The U.S.C. is a consolidation and codification of all the general and permanent laws of the United States in force on January 14, 1983. Title 18 is on Crimes and Criminal Procedure and Title 50 is on War and National Defense.

3. *Congress and the nation. Vol I. 1945–1964. A review of government and politics*. Washington: Congressional Quarterly, Inc.; 1965.

This is a summary of legislation and politics based on the *Congressional Quarterly Almanac*. This first volume covers twenty years, with tracings back to earlier years when required.

4. Ibid.

5. *United States Code*. Title 10, Chapter 37, 1982 edition. Washington: GPO; 1983.

The U.S.C. is a consolidation and codification of all the general and permanent laws of the United States in force on January 14, 1983. Title 10 is on Armed Forces, Chapter 37, Procurement Generally.

6. *United States Code*. Title 42, Chapter 23, 1982 edition. Washington: GPO; 1983.

The U.S.C. is a consolidation and codification of all the general and permanent laws of the United States in force on January 14, 1983. Title 42 is on Public Health and Welfare, Chapter 23 covers the Development and Control of Atomic Energy.

7. Executive Order 10104. *Federal Register*. 15: 597–598; 1950 February 3.

This Order on National Security Information was signed by President Truman.

8. Executive Order 12356. *Federal Register*. 47(66): 14874–14884; 1982 April 6.

This Order on National Security Information was signed by President Reagan.

9. *Congress and the nation. Vol. I. 1945–1964.*

10. Executive Order 10865. *Federal Register.* 25: 1583–1584; 1960 February 20.

This Order was signed by President Eisenhower.

11. *Congress and the nation. Vol. I. 1945–1964.*

12. Executive Order 10909. *Federal Register.* 26: 508–509; 1961 January 20.

This Order amends Executive Order 10865. Both were signed by President Eisenhower.

13. *Code of Federal Regulations.* Title 22 and Title 27. Washington: GPO; 1984.

Title 22 covers Foreign Relations and Title 27 is on Alcohol, Tobacco Products and Firearms.

14. *Congress and the nation. Vol. I. 1945–1964.*

15. *Congress and the nation Vol. III. 1969–1972. A review of government and politics during Nixon's first term.* Washington: Congressional Quarterly, Inc.; 1973.

This provides a comprehensive summary of presidential, legislative and political developments during the four-year period of 1969–1972.

16. *Congress and the nation. Vol. I. 1945–1964.*

17. Executive Order 12065. *Federal Register.* 43(128): 28949–28962; 1978 July 3.

This Order was written to balance the public's interest in access to government information with the need to protect certain national security information from disclosure.

18. Executive Order 12356.

19. Executive Order 12065.

20. *United States Code.* Title 35, 1982 edition. Washington: GPO; 1983.

The U.S.C. is a consolidation and codification of all the general and permanent laws of the United States in force on January 14, 1983. Title 35 is on Patents.

21. *U.S. Department of Defense Directive.* Number 5230.24; 1984 November 20.

This Directive applies to classified and unclassified information generated under DOD funding and is aimed at the control of U.S. generated information in science and technology, by the Reagan administration.

22. U.S. Department of Defense.

Chapter Four

Systems for Handling
Military Information

In discussing the specifics of systems used for handling military information there is a need to present descriptions of actual systems currently in use. Several organizations generously gave of their time and their knowledge to provide us with the information for this chapter. Their names have been omitted to protect their identities, but it should be emphasized that without their cooperation this task would have been nearly impossible.

President Franklin Roosevelt signed the first Executive Order on national security and information in 1940. Presidents Truman, Eisenhower, Nixon, and Carter issued orders in their terms of office. They dealt with what information was to be classified, the period of time, and the standards to follow. Each sought to preserve the free flow of information in the public interest, while limiting classification authority by defining the purpose and limits of classification, as well as procedures for declassification.[1] President Reagan signed Executive Order 12356 on National Security Information.

These Executive Orders set in motion the national security system for protecting the United States. Critical to the effectiveness of such a system is how it is carried out at the grassroots level within organizations. Such organizations are required to handle and use military information on a daily basis in order to conduct business which involves the United States government.

THE UNITED STATES GOVERNMENT AND
RESTRICTED INFORMATION

As discussed in Chapter 3, the Secretary of Defense acts on behalf of other government departments and agencies in the field of industrial security. In general, the same laws and directives that govern contractors also apply to these departments and agencies, although their internal systems may differ. Nonetheless, these organizations are held accountable for proper security measures in order to safeguard information. In addition, the Information Security Oversight Office (ISOO) ensures their compliance with the National Security Information program. These agencies and departments have their own security procedures specified in publications (for example, the U.S. Department of Commerce's *National Security Information Manual*,[2] or the *U.S. Army War College, Classified Document Handbook*).[3] Such manuals are in the public domain and are available for a small fee.

Classified information is not the only sensitive information that a government agency may handle. We can easily think of areas where every citizen is touched by information that is restricted, such as tax information handled by the Internal Revenue Service or census data gathered by the Bureau of the Census. In addition, a department or agency of the government may conduct some of its business involving proprietary information. For example, the National Bureau of Standards may do a study involving catastrophic failures, such as the collapse of a large hotel-entertainment complex, where proprietary information is involved. In such cases security is imposed to safeguard the proprietary data by limiting access to those people directly involved. The specific terms for security are worked out on a one-to-one basis by the company making the request along with the Bureau. The need for such security and the ramifications of inadequate protection are obvious.

GOVERNMENT CONTRACTORS AND
CLASSIFIED INFORMATION

Government contractors are organizations that do work for the government, on a contractual basis. In this case that work involves the national security of the United States and therefore classified information.

Such organizations may vary in size and their contracts vary in duration. Furthermore, it may include the contractor sub-contracting part of their effort to another organization. Generally, the nature of their work pertains to some aspect of defense, but it may include studies for state and local governments as well, be oriented toward non-defense activities, such as the environment or space research, and sometimes support direct profit-oriented businesses. In fact these organizations may be profit research facilities or the so-called not-for-profit research groups. In some cases they are governed and controlled through a typical management hierarchy of a business concern and in others through a board of trustees. It is not unusual that these research efforts are tied in with the academic community. They may be affiliated with one or a dozen universities, and generally their boards of trustees include personnel from the academic institutions involved as well as the scientific and technical institution itself. Such organizations remain separate from the government in order to maintain a research environment of integrity and independence.

When research or scientific and technical evaluations are performed for the U.S. government, specifically by the Department of Defense, their activities are regulated by the government. These regulations include principles for safeguarding classified information. The fundamental elements include facility security clearance, personnel security clearance, "need to know," and an internal document control and accountability system. These four concepts make up the system used for handling military information.

INTERNAL SECURITY AND RESPONSIBILITY

Within an organization (whether contractor or federal agency), responsibility for security and protection of classified data is a joint responsibility of the individual and the security operation of the organization, as focused in its Security Officer.

The guiding principle of any security system is that each individual is personally responsible for safeguarding classified information of which he or she has knowledge or custody. Furthermore, all employees are encouraged to have as few classified documents as required for their work. In other words, the material should be disposed of as soon as it has served its purpose and not be retained indefinitely. Such collections pose potential danger to the organization as well as the individual through loss or other problems related to accountability. Other major division, department, or headquarters' office heads are responsible for the personnel under them in their compliance with security measures.

As suggested, security responsibility for specific material (knowledge or custody) remains with the individual. However, the internal security system maintains a security operation with a security manager or officer at its head. These security managers have as their primary responsibility that of advising and assisting the individual in his or her compliance with national security regulations.

Organizationally, the security operation may be a part of the office of the head of the organization—the president, director, or other corporate officer—or it may be part of its technical or administrative operations. Usually, this is an arbitrary assignment having more to do with the players involved than with which area is functionally better, although there are contracts that specify what level or office is to handle security.

In support of internal security a document control and accountability system is an essential part of an internal security system. This may be a function of the security office itself, or part of the overall library or information center responsibility, or placed with a technical or administrative area. Again, this is fairly arbitrary but is most likely dependent on which other alternatives have been selected. One other point that should be remembered, an organization that uses classified information generates classified information and must account for what it generates in the same way as it accounts for what it receives from the outside, relative to the laws and the national security program. Most often, internally generated classified information is handled through the same system as that used for classified information received from the outside.

Facility Security Clearances

Every facility that makes use of or generates classified information must have a facility clearance. Such clearances are granted by the Defense Investigative Service after determining that the facility can properly safeguard classified information. This includes proper storage, such as vaults, file cabinets, controlled or closed areas, an employee identification badge system, a document control and accountability system, and other general security measures to monitor security in the organization.

Forms required for this procedure include DD Form 441 and 441-1, the Department of Defense Security Agreement and Appendage, which establishes the formal agreement that a facility will abide by the *DOD Industrial Security Manual for Safeguarding Classified Information*.[4] DD Form 254, Department of Defense Contract Security Classification Specification identifies specific items of classified information involved in the contract that requires security and is the basic document regarding security, and DIS FL 381-R, the Letter of Notification of Facility Security Clearance.

Personnel Security Clearance

Every employee must have a security clearance in order to work in a facility that has classified information. Furthermore, subcontractors, temporary help, and visitors who may reasonably be expected to be around classified information must also have a security clearance. Security clearances are granted by the U.S. government and are not usually given prior to employment.

Employees have personal responsibility for safeguarding classified information. This includes familiarity with security requirements and procedures relating to security guards, locks, combinations, vaults, alarm systems, closed circuit television, two-way radios, approved storage areas, and file cabinets in the facilities, as well as the control of information regarding proper classifications, downgrading, "need to know," and other control and accounting requirements of the material.

Forms required for personnel security clearances include:

1. DD Form 48, a Department of Defense Personnel Questionnaire, for Confidential or Secret clearance;

2. DD Form 48-2 for a Confidential Only clearance;

3. DD Form 48-3 for updating clearances, e.g., a transfer of employment from a user agency to an industrial organization;

4. DD Form 49 for a Top Secret clearance and other specific reasons related to the clearance. (See Chapter 3)

5. An Applicant Fingerprint Card, DD Form 258, required on each employee.

DISCO Form 560 is used to notify a facility of an employee's clearance, and DISCO Form 562 updates that record. Security Briefing and Termination Statements (for Industrial Personnel), DISCO Form 482, specifies the employees' knowledge of the provisions of the espionage laws and other federal criminal statutes regarding classified information. (See appendixes for extracts.)

Document Control System

The Department of Defense (DOD) requires contractor organizations to keep records at one or more control stations of the origination, receipt, transmittal, custody, reproduction, and destruction of all Top Secret and Secret material (this includes classified energy and NATO information), and all Communication Security (COMSEC) information regardless of classification. A record must also be kept of Confidential material that is received from and dispatched to outside sources.

As discussed earlier, responsibility for document control and accountability may be centralized or dispersed. For example, in some organizations Top Secret and Intelligence material may be controlled by the office of the head of the organization. In others, Intelligence material may be directed to one individual or one group whose primary effort is on intelligence, while Secret and Confidential information are put through still other separate points or combined and handled by one operation. In other cases no differentiation is made, and all such information is handled by one operation. This is often the library or information center, since their general activity is handling information.

Often the amount of material involved can be a determining factor on internal handling and of course the decision may be based on the director's personal predispositions. Remember too, we mentioned earlier that a contract may specify how classified information will be handled.

Most organizations have as a part of their control system organizational policies, security manuals, and handbooks that specify the procedures for accounting for classified material. These begin with broad policies, go to statements of requirements in compliance with the U.S. Security System, and end with detailed instructions at an operations level, specific to the nature of the activity of the organization.

The operations level will include a numbering system to identify each piece of information, not just that received from outside but including classified information produced inside. Additional copies, parts, drafts, photographs, or different formats, such as microfiche, are associated with the basic number as well. The number given follows the material throughout its lifetime in the organization until it is transferred to an external source or destroyed.

Such detailed measures are necessary when dealing with classified information. Every facility is inspected regularly by the regional cognizant security office and is held accountable for all classified information within the organization. This means that an inspector should be able to pull any record and track the document to the destination of the material or its destruction record. This tracking is carried out using the records of receipt, transfer, and destruction. If the trail cannot be followed and the material is not accounted for, a security infraction is recorded. If a sufficient number of items is not accountable, a major violation is reported on the organization.

There are facility violations (e.g., combination locks and records not properly handled) and information violations (e.g., documents not accounted for), which can jeopardize the government contract to the organization. Certain security violations can result in fines, imprisonment, or both to personnel (see appendixes). Such actions are not dependent on whether or not a person is a paid employee of that organization. Security violations are a federal offense.

INFORMATION AND ITS CLASSIFICATION

A great deal of the information used by an organization, even one engaged in DOD work, is unclassified; however, it is screened at some level before its classification is determined. In this section we will look at access to classified information and the types of classification it might have, and what that classification means.

"Need to Know" and the User

Before we look specifically at classifications we need to address two important principles in the classified information environment. First, the concept of "need to know." Position, title, security clearance, or senior rank does not grant access to classified information. The requester must have a personnel security clearance and the organization must be cleared as a secure facility, and he or she must also have a specific "need" for that information. In other words, the requester must justify by reason of his or her work that a genuine need for specific information exists. Second, it is the experience of the authors, as well as those interviewed, that people do not ask for information simply because it is classified. They request information pertinent to their work. If anything, there is an attitude of not wanting to deal with or be responsible for any more classified information than is necessary for getting the job done.

Information Classifications and Markings[5],[6]

There are several different levels of classification for security information. In part it has to do with national security, but it may also be an indication of what is contained in the information, such as energy data. The classifications may be Top Secret, Confidential, Restricted Data, Formerly Restricted Data, NATO, CNWDI, Intelligence, CRYPTO, COMSEC, TEMPEST, and Foreign Government Information. A person may come in contact with some or all of these and others; however, these are the major classifications used to identify classified information.

Top Secret. This term is applied to information which, if released, could reasonably be expected to *cause exceptionally grave damage* to the national security. Examples of "exceptionally grave damage" include armed hostilities against the U.S. or its allies, disruption of foreign relations vitally affecting the national security, the compromise of vital material defense plans or complex cryptologic and communications intelligence systems, the revelation of sensitive intelligence operations, and the disclosure of scientific and technological developments vital to national security.

Secret. The unauthorized disclosure of such information could reasonably be expected to *cause serious damage* to the national security. Examples of "serious damage" include disruption of foreign relations significantly affecting the national security; significant impairment of a program or policy directly related to national security; revelation of significant military plans or intelligence operations; compromise of significant military plans or intelligence operations; and compromise of significant scientific or technological developments relating to national security.

Confidential. Confidential information, if released unauthorized, could reasonably be expected to *cause damage* to the national security.

In addition, certain information is provided security under the Atomic Energy Act:

Restricted Data. This marking indicates that the material contains Restricted Data as defined in the Atomic Energy Act of 1954 and that unauthorized disclosure is subject to administrative and criminal sanctions. These data concern design, manufacture, or utilization of atomic weapons, the production of special nuclear material, or the use of special nuclear material in the production of energy.

Formerly Restricted Data. Unauthorized disclosure is subject to administrative and criminal sanctions. It is handled as Restricted Data in foreign dissemination. This information is removed from the Restricted Data category upon joint determination by Department of Energy (DOE) and DOD that such information relates primarily to the military utilization of atomic weapons and that such information can be adequately safeguarded as classified defense information.

S-RD indicates the material is Secret—Restricted Data. C-FRD indicates the material is Confidential—Formerly Restricted Data.

Additional security markings and terms include the following:

Intelligence. Classified material that contains intelligence information. Such information is the product resulting from the collection, evaluation, analysis, integration, and interpretation of all available information which concerns one or more aspects of foreign nations or of areas of foreign operations and which is immediately or potentially significant to military planning and operations.

TEMPEST. This is an unclassified short name referring to investigations and studies of compromising emanations associated with information processing systems, as related to disclosure of classified information.

Sensitive Compartmented Information. This term refers to all information and materials bearing special community controls indicating restricted handling within present and future community intelligence collection programs and their end products for which community systems of compartmentation have been or will be formally established.

NATO. This term embraces all classified information (military, political, and economic) that is circulated within and by NATO whether such information originates in the organization itself or is received from member nations or from other international organizations.

NATO-R refers to NATO—Restricted Data, NATO-S refers to NATO—Secret, and U.K.-C reflects the country and appropriate classification—United Kingdom—Confidential.

CNWDI. Critical Nuclear Weapon Design Information is Top Secret Restricted Data or Secret Restricted Data revealing the theory of operation or design of the components of a thermonuclear or implosion-type fission bomb, warhead, demolition munition, or test device. Specifically excluded is information concerning arming, fusing, and firing systems; limited life components; and totally contained quantities of fissionable, fusionable, and high explosive materials by type.

CRYPTO. This is a marking used to identify all COMSEC (Communications Security) keying material used to protect or authenticate telecommunications carrying national security-related information. The CRYPTO marking also identifies COMSEC equipment with installed hardwired operational wiring variables.

Foreign Government Information. This marking is used on U.S. documents containing "Foreign Government Information" to ensure that such information is not declassified prematurely or made accessible to nationals of a third country without consent of the originator.

Some classifications require special access authorization beyond that of Secret or Top Secret personnel security clearances, for example NATO and CNWDI. In addition to classification markings, work done under a DOD contract that is to be published, presented at a meeting, or distributed to the public must be cleared before its release, according to DOD Directive 5230.24.[7] This includes classified and unclassified information. The following seven distribution statements apply:

Distribution Statement A. Approved for public release; distribution is unlimited. This statement may be used only on unclassified technical documents that have been cleared for public release. Such documents can be sold and exported.

Distribution Statement B. Distribution authorized to U.S. government agencies only (fill in reason) (date of determination). Other requests for this document shall be referred to (insert controlling DOD office). Reasons for assigning this distribution statement include: (1) Foreign government information; (2) Proprietary information; (3) Test and evaluation; (4) Contractor performance evaluation; (5) Administrative or operational use; (6) Software documentation; or (7) Specific authority.

Distribution Statement C. Distribution authorized to U.S. government agencies and their contractors (fill in reason) (date of determination). Other requests for this document shall be referred to (insert controlling DOD office). Reasons for assigning this distribution statement include: (1) Critical technology; (2) Administrative or operational use; or (3) Specific authority.

Distribution Statement D. Distribution authorized to the Department of Defense and DOD contractors only (fill in reason) (date of determination). Other requests shall be referred to (insert controlling DOD office). Reasons for assigning this distribution statement include: (1) Premature dissemination; (2) Software documentation; (3) Critical technology; or (4) Specific authority.

Distribution Statement E. Distribution authorized to DOD components only (fill in reason) (date of determination). Other requests shall be referred to (insert controlling DOD office). Reasons for assigning this distribution statement include: (1) Export limitations; (2) Foreign government information; (3) Premature dissemination; (4) Software documentation; (5) Critical technology; or (6) Specific authority.

Distribution Statement F. Further dissemination only as directed by (insert controlling DOD office) (date of determination) or higher DOD authority. This statement is normally used only on classified technical documents, but may be used on unclassified technical documents when specific authority exists.

Distribution Statement X. Distribution authorized to U.S. government agencies and private individuals or enterprises eligible to obtain export-controlled technical data in accordance with regulations implementing 10 U.S.C. 140c (date of determination). Other requests must be referred to (insert controlling DOD office). This statement is to be used on unclassified documents when distribution statements B, C, D, E, or F are not applicable, but the document does contain technical data.

In addition to statements that limit distribution of technical documents, they may also contain notices. A technical document that contains export-controlled technical data will be marked with a WARNING notice. "This document contains technical data whose export is restricted." All technical documents marked with distribution statements B, C, D, E, F, or X will be marked with DESTRUCTION NOTICE. Limited distribution reports require special procedures for obtaining them.

EDUCATION AND THE SECURITY SYSTEM

Any facility that has access to classified information must educate its employees in security matters. This begins at the time of employment when individuals are requested to read extracts from espionage, sabotage, and conspiracy statutes. The forms used refer to specific laws that govern the information each provides and the penalties involved as well as those laws that protect the information given.

Earlier chapters discussed specific laws, executive orders, and other legislation that govern the handling of military information. In addition the following directives and laws are also used by the organizations being dealt with here. These include DOD Directive 5210.2 for Critical Nuclear Weapon Design Information; DOD Directive 5220.22-S-1 for Communications Security (COMSEC); DOD Directive 5220.22, Department of Defense Industrial Security Program; DOD Directive 5220.22-C on Carriers; Privacy Act of 1954; and the Freedom of Information Act, Revised 1974.

The security manager is responsible for the development, direction, and administration of the internal security system in accordance with the *DOD Industrial Security Manual* and the policies of the organization's management, along with the cognizant government security and contracting offices. The manager is usually called upon for guidance in all security-related matters, irrespective of placement in the organization.

Training on in-house rules generally takes place after the individual is hired. This on-the-job training is usually accompanied by procedural manuals for security as well as operations. Briefings are also held for all employees to discuss specific concerns or changes to security laws and procedures. Procedures may change if the regulations are changed or if security proves inadequate under current rules. The Defense Investigative Service may point out problematic areas for the contracting agency during a routine inspection. Procedures will be changed accordingly. Security violations may be found by the inspectors which could and probably will affect the procedures currently in use.

Organizations handling classified information generally take that responsibility seriously. Thus an individual's non-compliance with security practices may result in disciplinary action by the organization, the government, or both and could result in loss of security clearance, suspension without pay, or dismissal.

REFERENCES

1. Rosenbaum, Robert A.; Tenzer, Morton J.; Unger, Stephen H.; Van Alstyne, William; and Knight, Jonathan. Academic freedom and the classified information system. *Science.* 219(4582): 257–259; 1983 Jan. 21.

Discusses President Reagan's Executive Order 12356 on National Security Information and contrasts it with previous Executive Orders and the implications, especially that which relates to academic research.

2. U.S. Department of Commerce. *National security information manual.* Washington: NTIS; 1983 Mar. 4; PB83-187765; DAO-207-2. 64p.

Addressed to all Department of Commerce units, committees and offices and specifies policies and procedures for safeguarding national security information within the DOC.

3. U.S. Army War College, Security Division. *Classified document handbook.* Washington: NTIS; 1983 Oct. 1; AD-A137-002. 16p.

Addresses the preparation of a classified document and is applicable to all components of the U.S. Army War College.

4. U.S. Department of Defense. *Industrial security manual for safeguarding classified information.* Washington: GPO; 1984 March; DOD 5220.22-M. 345p.

Establishes uniform security practices as determined by the U.S. government.

5. Ibid.

6. U.S. Department of Defense. *Industrial security regulation.* Washington: GPO; 1984 Feb.; DOD 5220.22-R. 255p.

Prescribes uniform procedures that ensure the safeguarding and protection of classified information made available to industry.

7. *U.S. Department of Defense Directive. Number 5230.24*; 1984 November 20.

This Directive applies to classified and unclassified information generated under DOD funding and is aimed at the control of U.S. information in science and technology, by the Reagan administration.

PART III
COMMERCIAL INFORMATION

Another person's secret is like another person's money: you are not so careful with it as you are of your own.

Edgar Watson Howe, 1911

This part concerns commercial information. Chapter 5 addresses a typical system for safeguarding vulnerable commercial data. Chapter 6 describes specific examples of the methods used to handle restricted commercial data.

Chapter Five

Safeguarding
Commercial Information

One of the most valuable assets of commercial firms is information. It might be in the form of so-called trade secrets (such as techniques or chemical formulas for making a particular product), or it might be data showing likely markets for a company's services and products, or it might be details of company strategy in regard to a forthcoming court case. Whatever the type of information, it is in the best interests of the commercial organization to ensure that access to sensitive information is limited only to those whom the organization wishes to have access. Great sums of money, perhaps even the existence of the organization, can depend upon a tight security system.

ESTABLISHING A SECURITY SYSTEM

Establishing good security measures for guarding commercial restricted information depends upon several factors.

A security system is doomed to failure if personnel below top management attempt to impose a system on higher-ups who are uninterested in or opposed to the proposed system. Some of the most sensitive information in an organization is often known only to a few of those in the top management category. If they disregard security precautions, it does little good to worry about what could happen at lower levels.

A good security system is not overly complex, but neither is it simplistic. So many types of company activities must be kept in mind when planning for security that it would be rare to find one or two employees who understood so well all the details of operation in each segment of the organization that they could design a good system by themselves. A much better plan would be to have consultations with representatives of each department of the company, with final approval given by a person high in the organization.

The best intentions and degree of cooperation one could hope for will still not produce an adequate security system if the one in charge is not first rate in ability. Some security managers may have a blind spot as far as more sophisticated problems involving protection of data, particularly when computerized data files are involved. Some managers may be out of touch with the electronic age and allow systems to be put in use which can easily be penetrated by a clever person used to working with computerized data. Some companies allow this task to be assigned on a casual basis, perhaps to an overworked office manager because he or she handles records, or to some supervisor who is perceived as not having enough to do each day. Even worse are those firms that have no one person in charge taking an overview of the entire security problem.

Credentials in many organizations for the position of manager of security systems are nearly as vague as those for manager of information services or head of the records management program. In the case of security there are professional organizations from which to draw, such as the American Society for Industrial Security. More than one security manager was formerly an FBI agent or police officer. One danger is that of hiring a person to protect the physical security of a building or laboratory who is not capable of protecting written and recorded data. At any rate, management of security is not a job to be handed out to just any employee.

Before any large-scale security program can get underway, an audit or survey must be made to find out what types of data need protection. This would include determining what type of protection is needed. For example, a firm with a very valuable set of drawings and reports describing in great detail a particularly complicated and vital manufacturing procedure would want to give more protection to that than to sales figures or some lesser topic.

Needless to say, the survey must be done thoroughly, then put to scrutiny by a group of supervisors representing all departments having sensitive materials. A good survey leaves out nothing, not even a seemingly minor detail like the method used to empty wastebaskets. More than one security loss has occurred because outsiders had access to trash collections, which sometimes included drafts or carbon copies of important documents.

For best results all employees must be instructed in company security procedures at the time of hiring, with periodic refresher sessions. Security is no better than the average person's acceptance of the need for security and cooperation in carrying out procedures. Obviously there is no guarantee that each apparently trustworthy employee is actually cooperating, but the design of the security system should make it very difficult for any employee to evade security measures.

One way to ensure that all employees understand the operation and purpose of a company security system is to prepare a security manual, distributed to all employees and updated as needed. Later in the chapter this will be discussed at more length.

VULNERABILITY OF COMMERCIAL DATA

There are many reasons for unscrupulous people to seek out commercial data. An article by Augenblick lists a rather disturbing number of possible agents of industrial espionage:[1]

- foreign agents seeking data for their own countries,

- competitors seeking data for U.S. firms,

- suppliers seeking data to help them get an advantage in bidding on contracts,

- certain employees seeking data from management circles to further their own careers,

- traders in stock seeking data to help them gain profits in trading,

- information brokers seeking data for sale to competitors,

- activists seeking data to embarrass a company over its policies in certain matters, and

- terrorists seeking data to aid them in committing acts of violence against the company.

No doubt one could list several other reasons for people to seek illegal access to commercial data of one sort or another.

An article by Blanchard points out that one of the chief tools for getting illegal access is the "bug" or microtransmitter.[2] Due to advances in microelectronics, these devices can be made so small that they are difficult to detect except with sophisticated electronic equipment. The bug is powerful enough to transmit even whispered conversation taking place in a room for distances of several hundred yards away, where an agent can record what is being said. Another powerful device is the portable laser, one use of which is to interpret the vibrations of glass in a window caused by conversation going on in the room. The output of the laser can be converted back into sound so that an agent as much as five-hundred yards away can listen to the conversation.

As Augenblick points out, there are many myths about electronic eavesdropping, such as: you are not being bugged if your phone doesn't click; bugs are very difficult to obtain and install; bugs are easily recognized; nobody would want to bug your company; and only trained spies with years of experience would try to bug your operation.

COMPANY SECURITY MANUALS

As previously noted, some firms have developed detailed manuals prescribing steps to be taken within the organization for safeguarding sensitive information. An article by Dunlop cites examples from a manual prepared by Texas Instruments, an important firm in an industry where some of the most active industrial spying is apt to occur.[3] One section of the manual concerns physical security, listing such points as the location and construction of materials for exit doors or the conditions under which an employee identification badge must be turned back to security guards. The article is also illustrated with a section of the manual which shows the title of the person responsible for certain administrative duties, such as the amount of trade information that can be given to non-employees (head of the corporate legal activity) or the identification of employees with a "need to know" for certain projects (security monitor for projects). Such a publication, while not to be heralded as a guarantee of secure conditions at a company, would undoubtedly result in much better security than if there were no formal manual.

Many ideas for reducing security losses or compromises that might well be incorporated in a company manual are to be found in an article by Menkus.[4] Some of his points concern the need to destroy used carbon paper or used typewriter and computer printer film ribbons, or the need to change combinations of locks on rooms or containers housing sensitive documents. In addition the author gives advice on how to prevent unauthorized use of lists of companies or suppliers, data which could be very valuable to competitors. The article also includes a typical agreement which employees could sign regarding nondisclosure of information, a vital matter that must not be overlooked.

SURVEY OF ATTITUDES

An interesting set of surveys concerning executives' attitudes towards illegal information gathering is discussed in an article by Wall.[5] He compares a survey made of company executives in 1959 with one he made in 1973 of more than 1,200 industrial leaders. His findings shed light on opinions held on a variety of topics:

- Most executives assume industrial espionage has increased.

- The level of interest has increased in all types of data, depending upon the industry involved and the size of the company.

- Few firms are using formal methods of gathering data on competitors, although many of them feel they should be doing more.

- Hiring a competitor's key employee is increasing in frequency as a means of gaining information.

- Larger firms are using more security measures than small ones.

- Very few of the respondents reported they would use illegal or immoral means of gaining data from competitors.

A SYSTEM FOR HANDLING COMMERCIAL INFORMATION

It is not uncommon for managers of special libraries or information centers to find themselves suddenly given the extra responsibility of managing all or a portion of company proprietary data, such as reports, laboratory notebooks, or even correspondence. An article by Graham may aid newcomers in this situation as she describes in considerable detail the problems of establishing a system for the organization and handling of such materials.[6] She points out that although many librarians have no great desire to take on new types of materials, this sort of assignment should be seen as an opportunity to expand the value of the library and to increase the number of users served. Her recommendations for creating a system supplement the list of elements of a system found in Chapter 1.

To summarize the elements of a system for handling proprietary information, she names the following points:

- Identify the kinds of materials to be included in the system.

- Arrange for documents to flow into the system from individuals and departments of the organization.

- Select an indexing system for the documents.

- Overcome resistance of individuals to a new system.

- Establish a retention policy for all types of materials in the system.

- Allow for storage and availability of all documents in the system, including use, where appropriate, of microforms and digital storage.

- Establish a means for retrieving documents by several types of tags, such as subject, author, date, type of document, and so forth, as well as a means of alerting users to new materials of interest that are being added to the system.

Graham points out the need for educating management to the benefits of assigning responsibility for handling proprietary materials to the library or information center, rather than to other organizational units not geared to the principles and techniques of dealing with informational materials.

There is a substantial amount of literature that could serve those new to the problems of handling proprietary literature. For example, an issue of a journal devoted to science and technology libraries contains one paper on the problems and techniques of handling laboratory notebooks along with two papers which discuss how two major research organizations, Bell Laboratories and the Exxon Research and Engineering Company, each have developed modern computerized systems for dealing with company reports.[7] Other examples can be found for guidance in the handling of proprietary materials.

COMMERCIAL VERSUS ACADEMIC VIEWPOINTS

It should not be surprising that government, commercial, and academic leaders have differing viewpoints about the type and amount of information that should be restricted. Even the academic community is by no means in agreement on these matters. For example, the attitudes of university and college administrations and faculty towards military information vary from school to school. As was pointed out in an earlier chapter, many academic institutions will not allow any classified military contracts to be pursued on their campuses. A few take a slightly less rigid position, and they allow university-sponsored institutes, often not on the campus itself, to engage in classified military contracts.

However, there is much more agreement among schools in regard to involvement with commercial data. There are far fewer instances of an outright ban on such agreements being pursued on campuses. Many universities, for example, have contracts to do research for commercial firms, including those which allow the schools the right to partial or complete ownership of patents developed during the projects, patents which in some cases are significant sources of funds for the schools. There is little or no campus resistance to such sources of income. The one issue that does raise the hackles of many professors and staff researchers is that of attempts by the federal government to confine the dissemination of unclassified research findings done without commercial sponsorship.

To most academicians there is no question that they have the right to distribute anywhere in the world the findings of research done without government or commercial backing. As understandable as this might be as a traditional viewpoint of the academic world, this position is not favored by many business executives, who must face restrictions imposed by the government, including the sale abroad of certain sensitive products. An article by Wallich reports one business leader as saying, "There has been a dual standard. Universities have had relatively little government control of information, while companies have had a great deal."[8] Yet this same person has recognized the possible effects of greater restrictions on universities, stating this situation "would constrict the free flow of information between companies and universities; we'd be shooting ourselves in the foot."

Wallich's article also quotes a government official who states that efforts by the government to limit the flow of academic information abroad would concentrate on universities dealing with the transmission of proprietary data to Communist countries; government officials believe this requires applying for an export license, the same as industrial and business firms must do. This government official states that the federal government has no intention of trying to restrict the flow of information about basic research.

At any rate, most academic officials are not taking for granted the continuation in the future of their present freedom to disseminate most information without controls. They feel it is likely that more government action in this field will occur.

REFERENCES

1. Augenblick, Harry A. The "bugging" of corporate America. *Chief Executive*. No. 20: 21–23; 1982 Summer.

Describes the reasons for electronic eavesdropping, the nature of "bugs," and how they are employed.

2. Blanchard, Robert. Open season on company secrets. *International Management*. 35(2): 34, 38–39; 1980 Feb.

Describes the ways in which "bugs" are used and how they can be detected.

3. Dunlop, William C. Safeguarding trade secrets: one company's guide to protecting proprietary information. *Security Management*. 27(7): 44–48; 1982 July.

Discusses a company security manual prepared by Texas Instruments for its employees. Includes sample pages from the manual.

4. Menkus, Belden. Management's responsibilities for safeguarding information. *Journal of Systems Management*. 27(12): 32–38; 1976 Dec.

Defines types of business data to safeguard then discusses ways to protect such material.

5. Wall, Jerry L. Probing opinions: a survey of executives' attitudes, practices and ethics vis-a-vis espionage and other forms of competitive information gathering. *Harvard Business Review*. 52(6): 22–38; 1974 Nov.–Dec.

Compares surveys of business executives made in 1959 and 1973 regarding their attitudes towards ways of getting information about competitors, the amount and types of information gained, and the outlook for such activities in the future.

6. Graham, Margaret H. Management of proprietary information: the trials and the treasures. *Special Libraries*. 73(4): 280–285; 1982 Oct.

Examines the pros and the cons of being responsible for proprietary information in a special library or information center. Includes attitudes of information professionals as well as corporate management.

7. Role of technical reports in sci-tech libraries. *Science & Technology Libraries*. 1(4): 1981 Summer.

Discusses how scientific and technical libraries handle technical reports, including two major corporate libraries. Includes a paper on handling laboratory notebooks.

8. Wallich, Paul. Technology transfer at issue: the industry viewpoint. *IEEE Spectrum*. 19(5): 69–73; 1982 May.

Describes the efforts and outlook of the federal government regarding restrictions on unclassified information in the hands of businesses and universities. The types of controls being considered are also discussed, as are the attitudes of business executives towards academic practices.

Chapter Six

Systems for Handling Commercial Information

There is a general recognition of the need for safeguarding trade secrets; most people readily see the necessity for a certain amount of secrecy in the free enterprise system. However, people handling business information may not have had much if any training or guidance in the best ways to establish and operate suitable systems for restricting commercial information of this type. The systems and procedures described in this chapter should give readers some ideas for local adaptation.

Much of the data for this chapter was provided by cooperative business firms, who generally wish to remain anonymous. Consequently the chapter merely cites possible organizations where various practices and procedures might be feasible without actually naming them. Not surprisingly, different types of businesses have different types of information to restrict and different methods of doing so. Some have as much concern about controlling the flow of information within their firm as they have about access by outsiders.

FINANCIAL OPERATIONS

Many companies are concerned with corporate financial matters, such as the selling of bonds for manufacturing companies or the selection of likely companies for merging with other firms. In such organizations there is a great need to protect data on proposed mergers or bond offerings from outsiders, but what may not be generally recognized is the need to keep certain data from reaching those working in other departments of these companies. It is obvious why this is a problem—a person with advance inside information that Company X is about to buy Company Y in a move that would profit both firms would then be in an excellent spot to use this information to buy, or advise others to buy, stock in the companies affected. It is clear why the Securities and Exchange Commission keeps watch over the stock markets so as to detect the improper use of information of this sort. Those foolish enough to try to obtain and use data of this sort are usually caught, facing prison terms and heavy fines. Thus the confidential documents involved in these firms must be kept secure from both internal as well as external leaks.

One prominent company which deals in this aspect of finance has a security system with the following characteristics:

1. Departments which have the greatest concern about security of data (hereafter termed "sensitive data departments") are on separate floors or are in separate areas not accessible to employees from other departments or to outsiders. Anyone venturing into such areas would immediately be identified as not belonging there.

2. No markings of documents are used in the sensitive data departments in view of the fact that practically everything in the department dealing with, say, proposed mergers would automatically be kept under control by the department.

3. These sensitive data departments often have their own libraries for certain types of materials not safe to put in the regular company library files.

4. The destruction or purging of certain documents, after their legal and practical needs have been served, is handled by the sensitive data departments more or less independently of procedures established for handling records kept by other departments. The same would hold for sending materials to the company archives—the sensitive data departments send very little to the company archives, despite the tight control maintained by the archives unit and the existence of an elaborate scheme of categories available to aid quick retrieval of materials in storage.

5. Computerized systems in use in the sensitive data departments are wired directly to the company computer, with dial-

up telephone access not available. This would tend to make unauthorized access to the computer files more difficult.

6. The removal of documents for home use by employees in the sensitive data departments is discouraged, if not actually prohibited.

As can be seen, this company relies on limitations of physical access to the records for most of its security, as well as precautions against unauthorized electronic access to data. By isolating the sensitive data in small departments, the need for elaborate marking systems and control of who has what documents is probably unnecessary. However, some businesses have so much data to control that physical isolation would not be feasible. This company has tight security for access to any part of its office space, beginning at the lobby, and maintains careful control over less sensitive data by requiring that only authorized people have access to unpublished data kept in its regular library. Archival material is released only to the departments which sent it there originally. Security is given considerable emphasis in a business of this type.

ACCOUNTING DATA

Companies which provide accounting, auditing, and tax services on a fee basis for clients understandably deal with a great deal of confidential data. Improper disclosure of certain sensitive information about an audit or ongoing tax matter could have serious repercussions, affecting the standing of a client company, including adverse effects on its stock. Government regulations regarding improper handling of accounting data are stringent, adding another incentive for firms who provide this sort of service to exercise great care in handling restricted information.

Categories of Materials

One firm has three basic categories of restricted data:

Working Papers

This category includes documents associated with projects being carried out for clients. Little more can be said about the working papers aside from the fact that they are given careful treatment, with a minimum of access within the company. This material is kept in a vault, entirely separate from the firm's library or information center. Only those involved with the work for clients have access to such papers.

Confidential Documents

Included here are memos of an extremely confidential nature. These are distributed on a very limited and controlled basis, usually only to upper management.

Less Sensitive Materials

This category consists of several types of materials, some given more restricted distribution than others. The types of materials in this category are internal publications (internal information, guidelines, policies, etc.; information pamphlets, client marketing brochures; and user's guides, worksheets, etc.) and selected external publications produced by various professional organizations, such as the American Institute of Certified Public Accountants (AICPA), the Financial Accounting Standards Board, and so forth, which would include exposure drafts and final versions of accounting and auditing rules.

As can be seen, the last category consists of materials which range from sensitive internal guidelines and policies to items which could be freely circulated to anyone, such as marketing brochures.

Handling Less Sensitive Materials

The firm has a well-organized retrieval and indexing system for the distribution of these documents. There is a national office where most of these materials are printed and controlled. All its offices in different cities have a publications and retrieval file area to which copies of the documents are sent. These file areas provide copies of documents for employees authorized to see them. The larger offices have a formal library or information center in which the publications file is located. A non-circulating file copy is maintained in each retrieval file.

A system for keeping employees aware of what has been recently published consists of a weekly list sent by the central office to each employee on a professional level. Those seeing a notice of a new item for which they were not on the original distribution list may obtain a copy at the local library or information center or from their office retrieval file. Such collections are kept purged of obsolete documents by means of notices sent from the central office on an annual basis, following a review of all items. These lists authorize the removal of outdated material. Additional purge lists are released as necessary throughout the year in order to keep the file as up-to-date as possible. These purge lists also serve individuals who wish to keep their personal files of documents free from obsolete material. The national office keeps a file of "hard copies" of all purged documents.

As an aid to locating documents in the system, the central office also publishes an annual index enabling one to locate internal documents by subject and serial name, such as Tax Notes; external documents are searchable by issuing agency and by subject. This index, which is updated with a supplement six months after its issuance, is arranged by main indexing terms, followed by a brief description of the documents and their retrieval numbers. Each main indexing term is followed by a listing of related terms that could be useful. For example, the main indexing term of Life Insurance might be followed by a reference to Estate Planning and Group Life Insurance. In addition the system includes a use of such indexing aids as "See" and "See From." The system is based on an extensive thesaurus that was originally established at Price Waterhouse in the early seventies and was subsequently made available to other CPA firms through the AICPA.

The degree of confidentiality and the distribution approved for a document is indicated in writing on each document. In addition each document in the system bears a unique number; it consists of a notation that identifies the issuing department followed by a sequential number. In some cases, the document number may include a letter, a simple device for expanding the set of numbers available, also referring to the originating department.

The care given documents has resulted in a well-organized system in which awareness of current documents and retrieval of older materials are both taken care of in an efficient manner. The firm's system also provides for tight control of all documents of a sensitive nature.

LEGAL DATA

Law firms have a long tradition of handling sensitive information with great care and discretion. Lawyers have always maintained strict confidentiality of information given them by clients, akin to doctor-patient relationships. In small law firms practically everything is under careful scrutiny, and ordinary procedures in such offices prevent outsiders from gaining access to private papers of the firm. Locked filing cabinets are routinely used, and there are virtually no security problems unless by some chance some information sought by outsiders, ready to use illegal means of access, were to come into the firm's possession. In that case the firm's simple security methods would not withstand a skilled invader. This, however, rarely happens.

As law firms get larger, security becomes more of a problem. For one thing, there are more people around during the day to get access to papers they should not see. For another, the larger the firm the more likely it will be involved in matters of greater consequence, whether financial, political, or personal in nature. There is more incentive for an outsider to seek the data.

Each law firm has its own methods of safeguarding sensitive material. One method used by all is simply to be so aware of the presence of a stranger that he or she would be immediately noticed if attempting to enter areas where materials are filed. Even to enter such rooms is not easy with receptionists at all points of entry. Besides physical surveillance, many law firms routinely indoctrinate their employees in the need for security, with refresher sessions held periodically.

Files showing documents currently involved in litigation are particularly sensitive. Many are simply in standard printed form, but more and more firms are computerizing them. One firm with an online litigation file has a separate room, access to which is limited to the supervisor, and the clerical assistants, and only those attorneys listed as eligible to get material on certain cases. Blanket access is given only to the senior partners. Thus barriers to physical access are the main line of defense. How much difficulty a professional intruder would have in an afterhours attempted entry would no doubt depend upon the extent of use of alarms for the file area.

At any rate, security measures are commonplace in law firms; the larger ones have more to be concerned about and do take more stringent measures than smaller firms.

SCIENTIFIC AND TECHNICAL DATA

Restricted information often involves scientific and technical data. Such material can be of crucial importance to industrial and research organizations; it could include notebooks recording laboratory research, designs of equipment or processes, charts or formulas, and other documents. Such data have great immediate potential value in many cases, so it is understandable that scientific and technical organizations must use care in handling proprietary data, particularly when there is a strong demand for information on certain topics. Industrial espionage is only one means often used to obtain restricted information. Success in procuring stolen scientific and technical information can bring immense profits in underworld operations, even in so-called legitimate businesses.

Information on this category of restricted information was gathered from a number of scientific research laboratories and engineering firms. Some still used certain manual methods of handling data, while the others make extensive use of computerized systems for this purpose, often using programs prepared by their own employees.

In each case there is careful attention paid to security, beginning at the registration desk. Visitors must register and then await an escort to take them to the departments to be visited; no outsider just walks unaccompanied into or around the various offices and laboratories.

In general it can be said that restricted information in these organizations is restricted because of either military or commercial security regulations.

The first category is handled in appropriate chapters in this book; this chapter is concerned only with commercial restrictions. Note that of all the types of organizations discussed in this chapter, it is generally only those located in scientific and technical organizations which are very likely to be involved with both military and commercial restricted data; for example, it would be a rare law firm or accounting firm which became involved in such a situation.

In regard to commercial restrictions, there are, of course, different levels of restrictions. Some documents are freely available to employees, although such information usually cannot be passed on to outsiders. More sensitive information requires a "need to know" on the part of employees wishing to see the data, much like the requirements for data restricted for military security reasons.

In some cases the systems for keeping track of the eligibility of employees to see particularly sensitive materials is done on a manual basis, with lists of authorized persons available in document or library units; lists of supervisors or managers eligible to authorize access to documents are also maintained. In other cases most, if not all, of the checking of personal eligibility to see particular documents is now done on computers. However the records are handled, they obviously need to be kept up-to-date, quickly showing new employees or changes in the location or status of established employees.

In a typical case the computerized files contain the name and employee number of each employee, along with a listing of the projects for which each person has established a "need to know" entitling that person to see restricted materials relating to those projects. At more than one organization employees may request items on terminals in their offices or on terminals in the libraries, where full size or microfiche copies are maintained.

The average system in a scientific and technical organization contains several types of materials reflecting items designed for different purposes. A summary of the types that exist consists of three general categories, bearing different designations in different organizations.

Research and Progress Reports tend to be aimed at those involved in certain specific projects and are rather formal in nature.

Internal Memoranda tend to be narrow in scope and are not as polished as the former category.

Technical Correspondence tend to be more ephemeral in nature, although they frequently contain vital landmark data, such as agreements, goals, and so forth.

As previously mentioned, there are some scientific and technical organizations which, for various reasons, have made little or no use of computers in managing their restricted documents. One reason for manual methods may be that the total number of such documents is small enough so that more sophisticated techniques are not considered cost-effective. Another reason may be that the organization's management is not as progressive and active in applying computers as it might be. By contrast, in several scientific and technical companies online catalogs have been developed, including citations for internal documents as well as references to books, pertinent journal articles, and outside technical reports. One great advantage of having citations stored in an online system is that there are many ways of searching the file, such as by subject, keyword, author, project number, or contract number. Programs for online systems might be written by staff members, or prepared by outside consultants, or purchased ready-made by the vendors of turnkey systems.

Some scientific and technical library and information centers handle correspondence, while others do not. When such materials are involved, it is necessary for decisions to be made about means of access or retrieval. Again, the choice must be made between manual and computerized systems. It should be noted that technical correspondence is commonly sent to an archives file when no longer needed in active work areas; however, it is generally still retrievable.

Legal requirements for many organizations virtually require that little or no weeding be done; the more important a document may be in future legal or technical discussions, the more imperative is the requirement for permanent retention of original documents. Many library and information centers regularly prepare a variety of publications and lists to keep users aware of new literature, including those that list internal company documents. Requests may be made for copies by several methods, depending upon the equipment and sophistication of the organization. Besides telephone calls or personal visits, one system involves simply sending the library a form indicating what is desired; either full size or microfiche copies are usually available in modern information centers. As can be seen, there are significant variations in the ways in which scientific and technical groups handle restricted data.

It should be noted that the methods used for safeguarding commercial restricted information are left for the individual firm or company to establish, unlike the military information, for which the type and method of protection are carefully spelled out by government regulations and laws. While this opportunity for creativity in the commercial world may seem welcome to those who prefer to devise their own systems, it may also lead to poor planning and poor implementation by those unwilling to address the need for more time and effort to be spent at safeguarding commercial data.

PART IV
COMPUTER
TECHNOLOGY AND
RESTRICTED INFORMATION

It is unworthy of excellent men to lose hours like slaves in the labor of calculation which could safely be relegated to anyone else if machines were used.

Gottfried Wilhelm Leibnitz, 1671

This part consists of two chapters relating to computer technology and restricted information. Chapter 7 deals with some of the common problems of computer technology and information access and control, as well as the specific area of commercial information. Chapter 8 discusses computer security and military information, as required by the United States government.

Chapter Seven

Computer Technology and Commercial Information

HISTORY OF COMPUTER TECHNOLOGY

Some years ago The Johns Hopkins University, Applied Physics Laboratory developed an exhibit dealing with the invention of the modern computer. In researching the major areas for the exhibit it was soon realized that it was necessary to expand this effort to the history of the development of mechanical calculation—beginning with the abacus.

> Since antiquity, men have tried to make calculations easier. They have devised systems of symbolic notation, such as the decimal system, to represent numbers. They have developed mathematical techniques and concepts, such as logarithms, to simplify numerical operations. And they have invented mechanical and electronic devices, such as the abacus and the modern computer, to help them make the actual calculations.[1]

Since this ancient beginning, modern civilization has had to cope with an ever-increasing complexity in the usage of computer technology. What began as a way to improve activities requiring rapid calculation, using such machines as the MARK I and the ENIAC, soon took on the aspects of the manipulation of data as we know it today.

The punched card and paper tape used early on as a means of getting information into and out of computers are still in use today. However, since the invention of the transistor in 1948 this "new" technology has increasingly made its way to our doorstep. Not only do we use it at work, we entertain ourselves with it, as well as manage the family finances and even the home environment, if we so choose. It is for these reasons that we must take a closer look at this technology, recognizing its benefits and handling the associated problems, specifically as these relate to the control of and access to restricted information.

INFORMATION AND SYSTEM REQUIREMENTS

Earlier chapters have dealt with commercial information and the methods and systems used for handling this type of data. While the use of computers is an integral part of many of those operations, we need to look more closely at the areas of security and access to commercial information, specifically what elements are involved when information is coupled with computer technology.

Many information systems were built originally as manual operations for collecting data. As computer technology advanced, so did the system, although not necessarily taking into account proper controls and safeguards along the way. As we advance still further, and home and personal computers are almost as prevalent as the family telephone or television, new problems and issues have emerged that must be taken into account.

Ideally, a system is approached in the developmental stage and proper precautions, safeguards, and security requirements are built into it. Objectives should be identified and plans made to meet those objectives. Grayce M. Booth[2] identifies implementation-specific objectives for a hotel chain reservation system that relate directly to the user requirements, for example, response time and system availability. The implementation-oriented objectives for the same system might include functions to be provided; response speed needed; availability requirements; integrity, security, privacy, and auditability specifications; degree of flexibility for change required; acceptable cost of implementation and operation (based on expected "return on investment"); and schedule for beginning operation.

For our purposes we look more closely at the issues of integrity, security, privacy, and auditability, still referring to Booth's work and the developmental stage or planning of an information system.

Integrity

Integrity requirements include data correctness and level of system availability. The higher the level of integrity, the more expensive the system. Therefore it must be decided at what level the system can function most effectively. For example, financial data tend to require a high level of integrity and an interactive reservations system must be available for most of the time.

Security

Security may be imposed because of legal constraints, contractual commitments, or the need to protect data and computer facilities. This type of information is not limited to financial data and may include U.S. government classified information or product-related data, available to users who have a "need to know," or research in areas of high technology.

Privacy

Such protection may be needed as a result of legal requirements or public sensitivity to the misuse of personal data. For example, financial, medical, and personal characteristics may be stored in databases. In some instances personal data are covered by legal requirements to allow access to and correction of misinformation by the person whose record is in question. Organizations are increasingly aware of the need for internal controls and methods of redress and have in some cases enacted such procedures.

Auditability

There may be legal requirements for keeping specific records for auditing purposes, and there are specialized accounting practices relating to auditability. Integrity and security are both related to auditability. The former can mean the accuracy of the record, and an audit trail should identify which transactions were initiated, who initiated them and what the results were in each case as one form of computer security. For this reason online applications may present less secure situations since they often leave no audit trail.

Data collection, requirements definition, and system analysis are front-end functions that must take into account the system requirements for properly handling and protecting the integrity, security, privacy, and auditability of the design of information systems. Without that attention the resulting system may be unsatisfactory.

Need for Computer and Information Security

The prevalence of computers and computer technology has already been acknowledged here, as well as the need for the proper design to ensure integrity, security, privacy, and auditability. These basic requirements in an information system take on more meaning when we look at specific data relating to commercial information.

Losses to the private sector resulting from white collar crime are estimated to be in the billions. The computer provides an even better method for criminal activity for those who would use it and it often leaves no trail in the process. The misuse of the computer may be carried out by an employee, a consultant, a high executive, or a competitor. Every industry is vulnerable.

One study[3] funded by the U.S. Department of Justice reviewed 372 cases of computer misuse in both industry and government. It showed seventy cases in banking, sixty-six in education, sixty-one in government, forty-six in manufacturing, twenty-eight in insurance and twenty-four in computer services. Other cases involved transportation, retail stores, dating bureaus, trade schools, utilities, communications, credit reporting, securities, petroleum, and others.

Vulnerability of the Computer

According to Bequai, there are five stages of vulnerability in computer operations. These include input, output, programming, usage, and transmission. During input fraudulent data may be introduced, current data may be altered, key documents may be removed, or any combination of these can cause a lack of data integrity. Such manipulation of input data can cause serious problems for an organization.

Output data may be stolen, for example, customer lists, personnel lists, trade secrets, marketing plans, projected earnings, and other protected, sensitive data. Such theft is often not limited to the involvement of an individual in the company but can include outsiders such as competitors, labor unions, professional criminals, or foreign agents.

Programming is the step-by-step instructions that the computer follows in carrying out a specific task. A dishonest programmer or consultant may alter the program, delete pertinent instructions, modify the program, steal or copy the program, or destroy or sabotage it.

Unauthorized usage usually involves an employee who misuses

the computer: one who uses the computer outside regular working hours or work requirements. Unauthorized usage may also involve non-employees or computer hackers—individuals who may see accessing computers as just a game. This can cost an organization money, since computer usage time is an expensive arrangement. Transmission of data is the stage where telephone circuits or teleprinter lines are used to transmit data back and forth between computers and remote terminals. Through penetration of time-sharing service bureaus, access may be gained to billing records, rate ledgers or general ledgers, from customer files.

Other vulnerabilities include computer browsing, wiretapping, bugging, electromagnetic pickup, between-the-lines entry, and piggyback entry. These and the vulnerabilities discussed above can be thwarted by security measures covering hardware, software, data entry, and transmission.

SYSTEM EVALUATION AND PROTECTION

Once one has realized the need for security and what the problems are relating to the vulnerability of the system, it becomes apparent that all facets of the system must be protected. This is not only hardware and software but also includes physical, personnel, and procedural protection.

The hardware configuration must provide stability and reliability, software design must ensure integrity, and personnel must provide individual accountability. Furthermore it is necessary to have operational procedures that insure data integrity and information control and a physical environment that minimizes unauthorized access along with secure communication lines and links.

Some companies have begun to conduct Asset Protection Overview surveys, using security consultant specialists.[4] Beck suggests that the survey may include:

1. Evaluation of existing corporate policies regarding protection of assets;

   • review of physical security—locks, alarms, and so forth,

   • evaluation of effectiveness of security guard operations,

   • review of personnel screening procedures,

- review of company loss prevention programs, if any, including educational programs regarding theft, pilferage, and other shrinkage.

2. Review of control system to analyze possible exposure to internal and external fraud;

    - controls over inventory and movement of raw materials and finished products,

    - analysis of records, systems, and accounting methods,

    - review of warehousing, traffic, and distribution controls.

3. Possibilities of commercial bribery, kickbacks, or receipt of bribes by employees for inferior merchandise or non-delivery of merchandise or services contracted at inflated prices;

4. Potential for payoffs in the area of shipping, receiving, and EDP centers;

5. Security of trade secrets to prevent the sale of confidential information, such as sources of supply, buyer mailing lists, prices, and other competitive data.

Such surveys require a multi-disciplined task force with specialized consultants in areas of accounting, engineering, EDP control, traffic and distribution, purchasing, auditing, electronic security, and law. More important than catching thieves is prevention.

After surveying an organization's assets, the next step is to design systems that are as fully protected as possible. Computer security in some or all of the areas surveyed can involve several layers of security control, including software and hardware (at different points in the system); these differ according to the system in use. The July 1984 issue of *Datamation*[5] reviewed several software products for use in computer security.

Some basic and minimal controls include identification codes and passwords that have a very large number of possible combinations, which reduces the chance for guessing correctly, thereby gaining access. Telephone lines may be camouflaged so that the existence of a computer port on the line is not obvious. Callback is also a telephone security technique—it allows a person to answer several questions including his or her telephone number and the computer verifies whether or not authorization is granted. Communication logging may also be used, to a greater or lesser extent, depending on the system used, to log access attempts and monitor usage. Checking out a computer system and determining where problems may exist can be done through the process of risk analysis. It can be used in any of the areas identified above, as part of the survey of assets; however, here we will look at risk analysis relative to computer software.

There are, obviously, limitations with the methodology of risk analysis of computer software. Mohr[6] includes the following:

1. The risk scenarios developed are limited by the creativity and ingenuity of the team members and are not all inclusive.

2. Data regarding the probability of a fraud is limited and may be too imprecise to be reliable.

3. No reliable method exists for distributing the combined probability of a fraud over all the scenarios developed. Each scenario must therefore be given an equal probability of occurrence, which tends to overstate the identified risks.

4. Development of risk scenarios by a threat analysis team increases individual awareness of methods to circumvent existing controls and may increase the risk of a fraud occurring.

The asset survey has uncovered potential problems in the EDP center and associated computer technology. A person may further classify these into teleprocessing systems, systems that affect the general ledger, systems that update the physical inventory, and so on. Furthermore, each will be categorized by the function performed—inquiry, update (batch and teleprocessing), data entry, or data collection.

Ultimately, team members try to circumvent existing controls and do a detailed risk analysis on each system reviewed. Mohr identifies six major tasks.

1. Identifying control points within a work flow—from transaction initiation through computer processing and final disposition—for each major transaction type.

2. Developing risk scenarios that identify weaknesses within the current systems controls.

3. Determining possible loss from each scenario.

4. Establishing the probability that an identified scenario may occur.

5. Calculating an annual probability exposure value for each scenario.

6. Developing recommendations that, if implemented, may reduce the annual probability of loss.

This effort is aimed at evaluating the system and protecting it in order to control access to restricted commercial information. By surveying the assets of the organization and doing risk analysis of those areas that appear most susceptible to unauthorized access, management decisions can be made based on monetary risks relative to the costs involved in implementing the protective measures recommended.

Other Concerns

The four major areas of concern, or areas that require security, in any computerized information system are the human element, misuse of the system, industrial espionage, and natural hazards. The first three have already been considered, but it is equally important to note the natural hazards, including fire, water, wind, and earthquake, as suggested by Carlton.[7]

Fire is considered the most significant natural hazard to computer facilities since it can destroy data files and programs. Insurance may cover the hardware, but software and lost information may be difficult or impossible to reconstruct.

Water damage, a second hazard, may not harm such things as tapes, but it can do considerable damage to computer components and wiring. Water may come from floods, sprinkler systems for fire prevention, water pipes, or excessive moisture in the facilities.

Heat, associated with a fire or otherwise environmentally present, may also cause damage, especially to magnetic tapes. If the humidity is high, then damage may occur at lower temperatures. Accordingly, proper climate control equipment is necessary to protect both hardware and software.

Earthquakes, tornadoes, hurricanes, and loss of power for prolonged periods of time are other natural occurrences which can endanger the computer facility and its information. Although it is impossible to secure information totally, constructing well designed facilities, training personnel for emergency situations, and having auxiliary power sources can help insure against loss.

Other Protection

There is a growing awareness for computer security and especially protection of information. However, in the best of circumstances that protection may be inadequate, or a complete failure. A recent survey of one thousand major industrial firms that rely on computers for their day-to-day operations were asked how they would respond to a computer disaster. The results show that one third of the companies have done no formal research in this area and most have no plans to do so. Other findings show:[8]

1. More than 21 percent of the companies surveyed have no computer disaster recovery plan and no alternate arrangements of any kind.

2. More than 41 percent have some type of reciprocal agreement with another firm; that is, if one company's computer is. destroyed, it can run its programs on another company's hardware and vice versa.

3. Nearly 30 percent of the companies surveyed said they have another company's computer center available for use.

4. The remaining firms said they would turn to a service bureau to continue their operations.

5. Chief financial officers expressed a higher degree of concern about the possibility of a computer disaster than data processing managers, because of the former's greater realization of the company's financial dependence on the computer.

Even in those companies that have "arrangements," availability and compatibility is questionable, if the companies should be required to exercise their contracts. Excess capacity is not prevalent in data processing shops, and different operating systems on the same hardware pose additional problems.

Hoag notes that New York City's Department of Investigation has recently issued a manual of security procedures for the city's information processing facilities. It includes guidelines for establishing a disaster recovery plan. Two possibilities for such recovery are off-site storage and cooperative centers. Off-site storage is maintained for important information resources such as duplicate tapes and master files so that critical data—vital to the ongoing operation of a business—is not lost. More recently there has been a trend toward ventures in which a number of companies organize and share the cost of building and maintaining a standby computer facility.

DEFECTS OF SECURITY PROGRAMS

Bequai[9] identifies defects in four areas of computer security. These include hardware, software, data, and transmission. The defects are summarized as follows.

Hardware Security

1.   There is poor control of the data preparation equipment.

2.   Access to the system is poorly controlled (it is not limited only to those who "need to know").

3.   Transactions (or other fraud indicators) that have been rejected by the system are usually ignored.

4.   At least two people are not always present when EDP equipment is being operated.

5.   The computer operations are open to public viewing.

6.   System components are located next to open windows, doors, or outside walls.

7.   Overall operations are poorly supervised.

8.   Auditors have little or no training in EDP operations.

9.   Reports and other sensitive materials are discarded in outside (insecure) trash bins.

10.   Computer personnel are not periodically screened.

11. The system generates negotiable instruments.

12. The system is used to transfer credit, process loans, and obtain credit ratings.

13. Employee-management relations are poor.

14. Key responsibilities are not separated.

15. The EDP auditors played no role in developing the applications programs.

16. The industry is depressed, but the computer-generated data reflects record sales.

Software Security

1. Responsibilities for writing, authorizing, modifying, and running programs are not divided.

2. Computer operators are given oral (not written) instructions by programmers.

3. Programs do not contain a statement of ownership.

4. Threat-monitoring capabilities are not built into the programs.

5. Dubious deviations from the norm are not recorded.

6. EDP auditors are not consulted regarding needed tests and checks.

7. Responsibilities for program maintenance are not separated.

8. Audit trails of program changes are not maintained.

9. Program debugging is not separate from production.

Data Security

1. There is no accounting of documents that are sent for input processing.

2. Corrections on source documents are not accounted for.

3. Corrections on source documents are not made exclusively by the originating department.

4. Source documents are often discarded and are not kept for a sufficient period of time.

5. Payroll checks and other negotiable items are not numbered sequentially.

6. Purchase orders are not numbered sequentially.

7. Outputs are not logged and stored in a secure location.

8. Tape and disk libraries are not staffed or locked.

9. Accountability for maintenance of the library is not fixed.

Transmission Security

1. Machine-readable cards or badges that identify terminal users are not used.

2. Identification cards and badges are not collected at the end of the work period.

3. Passwords and security codes are changed only infrequently (or not at all).

4. Terminal users are not required to indicate when they will next become active.

5. Scramblers and cryptographic devices are not used.

6. Access by valid users to specific files is not controlled.

7. Unsuccessful entry attempts are not recorded.

The defects identified here, if considered prior to enacting an automated system, can protect the integrity of the data and control the access to restricted commercial and other types of information. It can help prevent theft, copying, or misuse of programs, theft of mailing lists, trade secrets, and other confidential data, and improve the security of the database from home computers, terminals, and other tools not properly authorized and controlled for interaction with the database.

COMPUTER SECURITY STANDARDS

The United States government, both civilian and military, as well as industry, has an ongoing need for computer security safeguards. Willis H. Ware[10] looked at the history of computer security, the need for security safeguards, and standards in a recent article. It is his view that industry and government have the same computer security requirements but that this is not well recognized.

The military has a long history of perceiving the threat against information and the damage unprotected information can cause. In contrast, civil government and industry do not share common ground, for these are diffuse organizations that lack the close knit community of the military.

The Department of Defense (DOD) has been the leader in the field of security, recognizing both physical and personnel aspects of security safeguards. It is now involved in certifying software—that it does what it is supposed to do and, perhaps more importantly, does not do what it is not supposed to do. Most such software is not classified, in the military security sense; however, it may be decided to classify software that is used predominantly to protect official state secrets.

Civilian government must also deal now with software security. The federal Privacy Act of 1974, for instance, improved record-keeping on privacy but also stipulates that an agency must take reasonable precautions to safeguard the information which it holds, thereby boosting the need for computer security.

In any event, the government will have to continue and perhaps accelerate its role in certifying systems. Two suggestions have been made in this area: use an already existing agency of the government that has the requisite skills, or set-up a multi-service agency operated and staffed by a contractor.[11]

The National Bureau of Standards, Institute of Computer Science and Technology (ICST) is also a key player in computer security for the government and is responsible for the Data Encryption Standard for the military, and more recently also the civilian government.

Ware suggested that the ICST be given full responsibility for computer security and developing a Federal Information Processing Standard (FIPS) that includes as well the administrative, procedural, and physical environments. He sees this as a unifying step in the civil government and a way to cause vendors to respond accordingly. Thus, business and industry will also be able to avail themselves of the same security safeguards and protect their information. To help in this area, NBS publishes a list of ICST publications dealing with computer security and risk management.[12]

COMPUTER SECURITY AND EDUCATION

There are several ways to keep apprised of issues related to computer technology and security. First, information professionals in general should become more familiar with all of the facets of information, attend professional society meetings, and read professional literature. The national library associations could benefit from interaction with security specialists such as the American Society for Industrial Security. Computer technologists would do well to increase their awareness of the traditional role of librarianship and its contemporary requirements in fulfilling that traditional role, as well as becoming more involved in the security issues related to computers, privacy, and the flow of information in society—military and civilian government as well as business and industry.

Numerous seminars are held dealing with such topics as security software, design of databases, teleconferencing, networks, management information systems, information and society, and so on. In addition, publications and films abound on security relating to personal computers, the minis, the micros, and mainframes, and networks, such as the *Computer Security Quarterly*, *Advances in Computer Security Management*, and *Time Bomb* (a film), and the *Computer Security Handbook*. There are also consultants who specialize in computer security and corporate information protection and conferences coupled with exhibits that center around computer security, addressing both hardware and software.

In essence, awareness is the first step to a secure computer system that will protect the data while restricting access and usage to those unauthorized. Certainly, the systems can and should be improved, however in each case the final determination is actually the people involved in the process. In a recent article entitled, "A Turning Point for Individuals and Societies"[13] it was pointed out that getting the public to understand and sanction, through peer-group pressure, the laws that govern, is the most effective deterrent to crime. If citizens respect the law, they will assist in its enforcement and computerized information systems will protect access to and control of restricted information.

A looseleaf service devoted to the problems of computer security has recently been published, covering a broad range of topics, from ways to decrease the likelihood of illegal access to a file to the use of an outside vendor's vault for safekeeping of crucial backup data.[14]

REFERENCES

1. Von Schulz, Jeanne V.; Kepple, Robert R. An Exhibit. "The Evolution of the Computer: from the Abacus to the Eniac." Johns Hopkins University, Applied Physics Laboratory.

This exhibit was the idea of Robert R. Kepple, Librarian, The R. E. Gibson Library, The Johns Hopkins University, Applied Physics Laboratory. Mrs. Jeanne V. Von Schulz, of the library staff, did the research, historical sketches, and selection of equipment associated with the exhibit. Besides the initial display at the organization, the exhibit was loaned to numerous schools, libraries, and national scientific and technical meetings throughout the United States.

2. Booth, Grayce M. *The design of complex information systems: common sense methods for success.* New York: McGraw Hill; 1983. 320p.

Emphasis is on systems design and analysis to better provide an organization with an information processing system that will fit comfortably into the organization. The author maintains that too much emphasis is placed on the technical details and not in defining what is needed.

3. Bequai, August. *How to prevent computer crime: a guide for managers.* New York: Wiley; 1983. 308p.

Deals with the full scope of the computer crime problem, including theft of high technology, international espionage and sabotage, takeover attempts, and even attempts on the lives of public figures. Some discussion is also included on the cashless society and problems peculiar to this phenomenon as well as inroads being made by the underworld.

4. Beck, Sanford E. Risk managers can help win the war against white collar crime. *Risk Management.* 28(8): 24–27; 1981 Aug.

Discusses the use of extensive surveying techniques in the prevention of white collar crime.

5. Troy, Gene. Thwarting the hackers. *Datamation.* 30(10): 116–118, 122–123, 126, 128; 1984 July 1.

Discusses computer port protection devices and looks at seventeen products from eleven vendors.

6. Mohr, Joseph H.; Ruckh, Patrick. Fighting computer crime with software risk analysis. *Journal of Information Systems Management.* 1(2): 9–17; 1984 Spring.

Looks at risk analysis of one organization's software systems from a potential cost/risk viewpoint in a quantified manner. Its purpose was to give executive management a sound basis for deciding how to control and protect business systems.

7. Carlton, John L. Security and computerized systems. *Management Accounting.* 55(8): 33–36; 1974 Feb.

Discusses the four areas of security required for an automated information system and the need for management to decide the amount of security needed and how it is to be provided.

8. Hoag, Ed. Safeguarding your computer. *Output.* 2(1): 28–32; 1981 March.

Looks at a data processing recovery plan to get a company up and running again when computer operations are unexpectedly disrupted by crime or disaster.

9. Bequai.

10. Ware, Willis H. Computer security standards for government and industry: where will they come from? *Computer Security Journal.* 2(1): 71–76; 1983 Spring.

Discusses the need for standards applied to computer security, not just for the military but also civilian government and business and industry, and suggests how this can be carried out.

11. Ibid.

12. National Bureau of Standards. *Computer Security Publications.* Gaithersburg, MD: NBS; (NBS Publications List 91) 1983 Oct.

Lists the Institute for Computer Sciences and Technology (ICST) publications dealing with computer security and risk management issues. The publications are available from GPO or NTIS.

13. Hill, Ivan. A turning point for individuals and societies. *Security Management*. 25(8): 116–117, 119–123; 1981 Aug.

Looks at common sense and everyday ethics and includes a copy of the American Society for Industrial Security Code of Ethics and Ethical Considerations, approved June 27, 1980.

14. Datapro Reports on Information Security. Delran, NJ: Datapro Research Corporation; 1985. Looseleaf; monthly supplements.

Provides current information on such problems as physical security, electronic data processing audits, disaster avoidance, establishment of access requirements, and risk analysis.

Chapter Eight

Computer Security and Military Information

GENERAL SECURITY REQUIREMENTS FOR MILITARY COMPUTER SYSTEMS

It is obvious that the requirements for computer security in handling military information are critical to the safeguarding of this level of restricted information.[1] Thus there are special security measures for automatic data processing (ADP) and word processing systems. Here the term ADP systems includes word processing systems and equipment. Such systems, when handling classified information, must also be provided with security features in the systems hardware and software design and configuration, as well as administrative, physical, personnel, and communications security controls.

While we are most interested in general purpose ADP systems here, it is not the only type of computer system the military is concerned with. Security measures for ADP systems associated with (or an integral part of) weapon systems, communications systems, tactical data exchange and display systems, or communications security systems fall under the provisions we are going to address. Security requirements are established with the design and development of such systems. Furthermore, additional specifications may be required by the contracting organization.

Generally, requirements are specified for the protection of information classified as Confidential, Secret, or Top Secret. Other types of classified information may require special access programs, beyond the requirements noted here.

A secure ADP system, with reliability and integrity features, has the following objectives: to avoid unauthorized (accidental or intentional) disclosure, destruction, or modification of classified information; and to avoid unauthorized manipulation of the ADP system which could result in the compromise of classified information.

In realizing these objectives the ADP system security controls should provide the following features:

1. Individual accountability. The identity of each user must be positively established, and his or her access to the system and activity in the system (including information accessed and actions taken), should be controlled and open to security.

2. Environmental control. The ADP system should be externally protected to minimize the likelihood of unauthorized access to system entry points, access to classified information in the system, or unauthorized modification of the system.

3. System stability. All elements of the ADP system should function in a cohesive, identifiable, predictable, and reliable manner, so that malfunctions can be detected and reported in a timely manner.

4. Data integrity. Each file or collection of information in the ADP system should have an identifiable origin and use. Access to, maintenance, movement, and disposition of information should be governed on the basis of security classification and "need to know."

5. System reliability. The system should provide each user access to all information to which he or she is entitled, but no more.

6. Communications security. Communication links and lines should be secured in a manner appropriate for the information designated for transmission through such lines or links.

7. Classified information control. Such information handled and produced by the ADP system, or stored on media for recording classified information, should be safeguarded as appropriate for the classification assigned to the information.

SPECIFIC SECURITY REQUIREMENTS FOR
MILITARY COMPUTER SYSTEMS

Prior to processing classified information on an ADP system, certain steps must be taken. These are necessary for gaining authorization for such work. It is the contractor's responsibility to meet the safeguard requirements for classified information in ADP systems and to ensure that approved security controls are in place and effective.

The approval (or reapproval) process requires that a request for processing classified information in an ADP system be submitted by an organization to the contracting security officer, for that organization. That request is accompanied by a Standard Practice Procedure (SPP) that describes the ADP system and the security controls implemented for it. These documents are used to judge whether or not authorization will be granted by the contracting security officer for an organization to process classified information. The contractor must appoint at least one ADP system security supervisor, and more, if additional facilities are involved or the responsibility for multiple ADP systems in one facility are too great for one individual. In the latter case, other appointed system security custodians may report to the ADP system security supervisor. Involved, as well, in this process is the establishment and maintenance of hardware and software integrity to ensure continued safeguarding of classified information.

If major system modifications are made, then an organization must request reapproval of the ADP system from the contracting security officer. Such modifications include: (1) major changes in personnel access requirements; (2) relocation or structural modification of the central computer facility or remote terminal facilities; (3) additions, deletions, or changes to mainframe, storage or input/output devices; (4) system software changes that have an impact on security protection features; (5) any changes in clearance, declassification, audit trail, or hardware and software maintenance procedures; and (6) other system changes as determined by the contracting security officer.

Security Modes

There are three ADP system security modes: (1) Dedicated Security Mode; (2) System High Security Mode; and (3) Controlled Security Mode. These are authorized variations in the security environments and methods of operating ADP systems that handle classified information. They are primarily defined by the manner in which the basic access requirements for user personnel security clearance and "need to know" are implemented for the system. Each may involve a varying mix of automated (hardware and software) and conventional (personnel, physical, administrative and procedural, and communications) security measures and techniques in discharging basic access requirements.

Dedicated Security Mode

All users with access to the system have personnel security clearance and "need to know" for all classified information contained in the system. Access personnel, administrative, physical, and communications security controls are established for the central computer facility; the ADP system's interconnecting communications links; all peripheral devices and input/output terminals; and areas containing remote terminals connected to the system. Controls must be applied to protect the highest classification category and most restrictive type of classified information in the system.

System High Mode

All users with access to the system have a personnel security clearance for the highest classification and most restrictive type of information in the system. However, some users may not have a "need to know" for all classified information in the system. Security controls are the same as those noted for the Dedicated Security Mode. Furthermore, additional controls identifying and separating users and classified material on the basis of "need to know" should be provided for in the operation of the system. These controls are handled through security measures in the ADP system's operating system and associated software. Again, the controls applied must protect the highest classification category and the most restrictive type of classified information in the system.

Controlled Security Mode

In this mode some users have neither a personnel security clearance nor a "need to know" for all classified information in the system. This mode provides a limited capability for the concurrent access to and utilization of the ADP system by users having different security clearances and "need to know." The lowest level of a personnel security clearance permitted in this mode is a Confidential clearance granted by the contractor. Security controls are the same as those noted for the Dedicated Security Mode. In addition, system controls consisting of hardware, software, and other appropriate measures are implemented to identify, separate, and control users and classified information on the basis of personnel security clearance and category of the information security classification. The controls for the central facility must be for the highest classification and most restrictive type of information handled by the ADP system. Remote terminal areas should conform to controls for the highest classification and most restrictive type of information, which will be accessed through the terminal under system restraints.

Personnel Security

The system itself must be protected, as discussed above, but security does not end there. Personnel is an equally important area relative to safeguarding classified information in the ADP system. Unescorted entry and access to the central computer facility and its components—such as areas housing remote terminals—should be limited to authorized personnel. These people should have a personnel security clearance and a "need to know" for the highest classification and most restrictive type of classified information they access under system constraints. The necessary personnel security clearance and "need to know" for ADP system users was identified above as part of the discussion on the security modes.

There are exceptions to personnel who do not require the same security:

- Personnel who receive output products from the system and do not input or interact with it otherwise (assuming the output is unclassified);

- Personnel producing applications programs and changes, or preparing data to be input to the system during classified processing periods (assuming that they too are working with unclassified products or data).

System support personnel and visitors must also be considered in the protection of an ADP system that processes classified information. System support personnel must have a security clearance commensurate with the highest classification and the most restrictive type of information in the system. This includes persons in the immediate vicinity of the system attending to the operation, control, and functioning of the system, as well as those persons who design, program, modify, test, or install system software. Access to specific classified information is governed by "need to know" in relation to individual duties and responsibilities.

Visitors, admitted to the central computer facility, should have a security clearance for access to the highest classification category and the most restrictive type of classified information contained in the ADP system, and a confirmed "need to know" by the ADP system security supervisor, or designated representative. This could include, for example, personnel for repairs and maintenance of the system. If such personnel are not properly cleared they may be escorted by the ADP system security personnel or a knowledgeable designated representative. One-time or infrequent visitors may enter the area with proper escort, if they are not allowed access to classified information or to the system hardware or software.

The contractor has the responsibility for indoctrinating ADP system users and support personnel in the need for sound security practices; the specific security requirements associated with the system in terms of system security mode of operation and user access requirements; the security reporting procedures in the event of system malfunction or security incident; and what constitutes an authorized action with regard to system utilization.

Physical Security

The physical security of the computer facility is as important as computer system security and personnel security. Generally, the physical security safeguards and access controls for the central computer facility and areas housing remote terminals, connected to an approved ADP system, should conform to those required for the highest classification and most restricted type of information processed by the system. There are exceptions, however, some of which are discussed later in this chapter.

Physical protection and access control for the computer facility and remote terminals may include the following.

1. Establishment of continuously protected areas with physical safeguards, depending on the overall physical security posture of the facility, the relative potential for unauthorized access, and the classification level and volume of the information to be protected. Structural safeguards should address

hardware, walls, windows, doors, door locking devices, ceilings, and other openings, such as ducts, pipes, registers, sewers, and tunnels. A level of collective controls should be established, which will ensure the detection of attempted surreptitious entry into the areas being protected. Thus, in the event of an unauthorized entry, the system and equipment can be inspected prior to classified operations.

2. Protection and control may be attained during working hours by the use of continuous surveillance by specific personnel that are cleared. These people should be physically able to exercise direct security controls over the system and the classified information being processed. Use of supplemental surveillance and supplanting devices may be used during working and nonworking hours. For example, use of alarms could extend the capability of the guards and, if connected to a central control station, supplant them. Furthermore, electronic, mechanical, or electromechanical devices may be used. These must be approved by the contracting officer but could include such things as a metal entrance booth with a combination on which the access control device is set to operate, and control cards.

3. During nonworking hours, protection and control may be attained through storage of the hardware and associated media in approved containers, where feasible. Approved containers could include GSA approved security filing cabinets or a Class A Vault. Such vaults are constructed under specifications that govern the floor and walls, roof and ceiling, vault door and frame unit, lock and locking parts, and miscellaneous openings, such as heating and ventilating ducts, pipes, and conduits.

4. Protection and control may be attained through establishment of closed areas for the central computer facility and remote terminal areas. Closed areas are separated from adjacent areas by a physical barrier capable of preventing unauthorized entry or observation by unauthorized personnel. Closed areas are constructed with specifications on hardware, walls, windows, doors, door locking devices, ceilings, and openings such as ducts, pipes, registers, sewers, and tunnels.

ADP system security controls can be adjusted by consulting the contracting security officer. Such adjustments can accommodate occasional Top Secret processing, periodic Secret or Confidential processing, connecting and disconnecting remote terminals, and word processing systems and equipment.

SOFTWARE AND DATA PROTECTION

System software used during classified processing periods must be safeguarded commensurate with the requirements for the highest level of classified information processed. Applications software, which in itself contains classified data or comments, or implements classified processes or algorithms, must be marked in accordance with classification procedures, discussed in earlier chapters. Unclassified or lower classified application software may be used during classified processing periods in accordance with specific security mode requirements and may be subject to additional conditions.

Input data, either unclassified or classified at a lower level than the highest level processed during a classified period, should be handled the same way as for application software. Standard contractor configuration control and software management procedures must be utilized to provide reasonable assurance for the integrity of the system, and be approved by the contracting officer.

Physical protection requirements for software and data may be satisfied by marking and safeguarding the respective storage media— such as computer tapes and disk packs—when the software or data can be determined to reside on specific media. Protection should be commensurate with the highest classification level of software or data.

TRANSMISSION CONTROLS

The transmission and communication lines and links between the components of the ADP system may transmit classified information under certain conditions. Transmission of such information between contractor facility complexes must be over approved cryptographic communication circuits. However, security contracting officer approval is required.

Transmission of classified information within a contractor complex may occur over approved cryptographic communication circuits, with the contracting officer's approval. If cryptographic equipment is not available, other approved circuits may be used, subject to the contracting officer's approval. Such circuits must be protected by an in-depth physical security system that includes dedicated lines, line surveillance, and physical security of the terminal stations.

AUDIT TRAILS

The general security requirement for any ADP system audit trail is that it provide a documented history of the system. An approved audit trail will permit review of classified system activity and will provide a detailed activity record. This can be used to facilitate construction of events to determine the magnitude of compromise, if any, should a security malfunction occur. To fulfill this basic requirement, audit trail systems, manual, automated, or a combination of both, must document significant events occurring in the following areas of concern:

1. Preparation of input data and dissemination of output data (that is, reportable interactivity between users and system support personnel);

2. Activity involved within an ADP environment (for example, ADP support personnel modification of security and related controls);

3. Internal machine activity.

The audit trail for an ADP system approved to process classified information must be based on the three areas noted above and stylized to the particular system. All systems approved for classified processing should contain most if not all of the audit trail records listed below:

1. Personnel access;

2. Unauthorized and surreptitious entry into the central computer facility or remote terminal area;

3. Start/stop time of classified processing indicating pertinent system security initiation and termination events;

4. All functions initiated by ADP system console operators;

5. Disconnects of remote terminals and peripheral devices;

6. Log-on and log-off user activity;

7. Unauthorized attempts to access files or programs, as well as all open, close, create, and file destroy actions;

8. Program aborts and anomalies, including identification, for example user/program name, time and location of incident;

9. System hardware additions, deletions, and maintenance actions;

10. Generations and modifications affecting the security features of the system software.

The ADP system security supervisor should review the audit trail logs at least weekly. Audit trails are retained for a period of one U.S. government inspection cycle.

COMPUTER SYSTEM SECURITY APPROVAL

As mentioned earlier, to obtain a computer system security approval, a letter of request is necessary, along with a Standard Practice Procedure (SPP) document to the contracting security officer. The SPP describes the ADP system and the security controls implemented for that system. Specific information to be included in this documentation is a description of the following:

1. The SPP for a system proposed for operation in the controlled security mode must also provide specific information required under the guidelines for the controlled ADP system security mode, as addressed in the *Industrial Security Manual.*

2. Personnel and physical security controls should be specified for the central computer facility, and for each area where a remote terminal is to be connected. Identification and control of all ADP system users should be explicitly documented, as well as control procedures for system support personnel asso-

ciated with the handling of classified information. Exceptions and adjustments concerning these controls should be indicated.

3. Hardware and software configuration and security controls used during classified processing are required. This should include device types within component sub-systems, both local and remote, and corresponding channel assignments; central processing unit model number and memory size; and whether the system is multiprocessing or using shared files or storage media. Device disconnects should be fully described.

   The capabilities offered to users, the system software used (with identification), as well as any security features coded in the application programs, should be described. All administrative and procedural controls, employed to ensure that hardware and software security safeguards are functioning effectively should also be included. Special modifications to the operating system should be specified and described.

4. Transmission controls should be specified. If the transmission is other than by approved cryptographic means, a complete description of the in-depth physical controls of the transmission lines should be included.

5. Administrative and procedural controls which address storage media clearance, declassification, audit trail, and other procedures should be specified in the SPP. Other specific procedures to include are as follows:

   • control, use, and maintenance of password files and privileges, including authentication of each authorized user;

   • summary of how, when, where, and why the system will be used;

   • access control procedures for the central computer facility and remote terminal areas;

   • methods and techniques to augment the system software to ensure the isolation of users with different levels of clearance and "need to know";

- if remote terminals are used, user sign-on and sign-off procedures and terminal identification techniques;

- storage and protection procedures for documentation files and input/output products;

- safeguards afforded system software while not in use;

- software test and verification procedures and records;

- normal and abnormal start-up, restart, and shut-down operating procedures; and

- controls for handling visitors and service technicians.

In addition ADP system security levels can be upgraded or downgraded. Such changes must be approved by the contracting security officer.

PROCEDURES FOR MEDIA AND EQUIPMENT CLEARANCE

To preclude unauthorized disclosure of classified information when changing the classification category or type of information to be processed in the system, each memory location, register, and other internal circuitry used for the storage of classified information should be overwritten or otherwise cleared of classified information before reutilization. This may be done by program instruction, clear switch action, power-on reset cycle, or a combination of these. The clearance action should be verified and recorded to ensure that all applicable portions of memory have been cleared.

Other storage media on which classified information has been recorded may be used for processing a lower category of classified information, or unclassified information, if overwritten once with unclassified information, or otherwise cleared (for example, power-on reset), and the action is appropriately verified and recorded. These media should be safeguarded as required for the highest classification of information ever recorded on them, until they are declassified.

Punch card or reader equipment must be physically examined as a part of the process of clearing the equipment. This may include visual examination of the normal card path through the equipment and the operation of the equipment for three or more card cycles with input hopper empty to detect the possible presence of punched cards which have not been processed.

MEDIA AND EQUIPMENT DECLASSIFICATION

The eventual release of a storage device or a system, including storage media, should be anticipated. Due to the physical properties and retentive capabilities of magnetic media and devices, special precautions must be taken in the release of such media to safeguard possible residual classified information, until the declassification procedures have been completed. Until all storage media and internal memory, on which classified information has been recorded, has been declassified, safeguarding requirements should remain at the highest category for handling classified information on such recording devices.

When such media are declassified and removed from the protected environment, a record of media declassification must be completed. This requirement can be met in the case of accountable media by completing a destruction certificate. For all other declassified storage media, a record of media declassification and release must be created and retained for two years after disposition of the media. Each declassification action must be verified and recorded, to ensure that all classified information contained on the device or component was totally eradicated.

Procedures for declassification of storage media and equipment are prescribed in the *Industrial Security Manual*. These include procedures for magnetic tape, magnetic disk, disk pack, and drum, ferrite core memory, plated wire memory, thin film memory, semiconductor memory, cathode-ray tube, magnetic storage for nondigital information, and printer ribbons.

These procedures can also be used for protecting commercial and proprietary information.[2] Bequai deals extensively with the problems related to computers and restricted information.[3] The information specialist would do well to use both the *Industrial Security Manual* and Bequai's text *How to Prevent Computer Crime: A Guide for Managers*, in addressing the problems of handling restricted information in an automated environment.

In addition, the contracting security officer should be relied on, as well, to provide direction, guidance, and assistance to the contracting organization in their handling of military information.[4,5]

There are several articles published on industrial security and ADP systems. Williams[6] includes security inspection check sheets for the individual and the organization in one such work. Such articles are indispensable when working out the details required in ADP systems in a secured environment.

REFERENCES

1. U.S. Department of Defense. *Industrial security manual for safeguarding classified information*. Washington: GPO; 1984 Mar.; DOD 5220.22-M. 345p.

The purpose of this tool is to establish uniform security practices as determined by the U.S. government. This manual is periodically revised to reflect the changes to the National Security Program.

2. Ware, Willis H. Computer security standards for government and industry: where will they come from? *Computer Security Journal*. 2(1): 71–76; 1983 Spring.

Discusses the need for standards applied to computer security, not just for the military, but also civilian government and business and industry, and suggests how this can be carried out.

3. Bequai, August. *How to prevent computer crime: a guide for managers*. New York: Wiley; 1983. 308p.

Deals with the full scope of the computer crime problem, including theft of high technology, international espionage and sabotage, takeover attempts, and even attempts to kill public figures. Some discussion is also included on the cashless society and problems peculiar to this phenomenon as well as inroads being made by the underworld.

4. U.S. Department of Defense.

5. U.S. Department of Defense. *Industrial security regulation*. Washington: GPO; 1984 Feb.; DOD 5220.22-R. 255p.

Prescribes uniform procedures that ensure the safeguarding and protection of classified information made available to industry. This manual is periodically revised to reflect the changes to the National Security Program.

6. Williams, Richard F. Computer/word processing security: how to obtain system approval and maintain effective security. *Classification Management*. 18: 94–103; 1982. Washington: NTIS; AD-A138-480.

Addresses computer security of ADP systems and includes security inspection checklists.

The unclassified journal *Classification Management* is published by the National Classification Management Society. This issue reports on their 18th Annual Seminar, 25–27 May 1982.

PART V
GOVERNMENT INFORMATION

A popular government without popular information or the means of acquiring it, is but a prologue to a farce or a tragedy or perhaps both.
James Madison, 1751–1836

Chapter 9 is devoted chiefly to a description of federal agencies which are important sources of information. Private sources for government information are also included, along with a brief description of sources dealing with local, state and international governments. Chapter 10 describes the way in which the Freedom of Information Act and the Privacy Act can be used for gaining access to certain types of government information. Next, conventional sources of information are discussed. The chapter ends with a review of major sources of state, local, international and foreign information.

Chapter Nine

Sources of
Government Information

UNITED STATES GOVERNMENT

The United States government is composed of three branches: judicial, legislative, and executive, all differing in terms of control and access to information generated.

Judicial Branch

The judicial branch has been considered, even recently,[1] as the most reluctant to make its information easily accessible to the average citizen. One reason given is that there is no demand, and another is that the citizenry cannot assess the *real* value of such information, relative to precedent and interpretation of U.S. laws and the justice system in general. Certainly, if there is any truth at all to this reasoning, it does not improve the citizens' understanding by restricting access to the information.

McCallum[2] identifies a number of tools for legal research and includes topical headings for Court Reports, Digests, etc.; Statutory and Administrative; Encyclopedias, etc.; Legal Research Handbooks; and Articles on Legal Reference in Non-law Libraries. The tools include those handled by the government and sold by the Government Printing Office (GPO), as well as those from commercial publishers of legal tools, such as West Publishing Company, Commerce Clearing House, Lawyers Cooperative Publishing Company, and Shepard's Incorporated. Many of those available, generally the more usable, commercial publications, are prohibitively expensive for the citizen and most general libraries, especially public libraries. Supreme Court sessions are published in the *United States Reports*.[3]

Legislative Branch

The legislative branch is reported on regularly in the *Congressional Record*. Meetings of the Senate and the House of Representatives have traditionally been open to the public, as well as their many committee meetings. Committee meetings involving comments from the public are published as "Hearings," a series of official publications.

Executive Branch

The most prolific source of information of the three branches is the executive branch. It includes not only the executive office itself (the presidency, the Office of Management and Budget, advisers, council and other units reporting to the White House) but also the major departments and agencies. Examples of some of these are discussed later.

Departments include Agriculture, Commerce, Defense (Air Force, Navy, Marines, and Army), Education, Energy, Health and Human Services, Housing and Urban Development, Interior, Justice, Labor, State, Transportation, and Treasury.

Table I (pages 132–133) lists Independent Establishments and Government Corporations.[4] A similar list entitled Independent Agencies is given in Table II (pages 134–137).[5] As can be seen from these two examples, different reference sources call government organizations by different titles and also include them according to differing criteria. In any event, it is important to note their inclusion as sources of government activity and therefore information.

Knowing the organizational framework of the government is necessary for retrieving information[6,7,8,9] in many subject areas. The purpose of a department or agency, for example, can lead the searcher to specific government information. However, it is equally important to determine methods used for retrieval, and the laws, regulations, and procedures that are often required as a part of that retrieval process, subjects dealt with in other parts of this book.

CABINET-LEVEL DEPARTMENTS[10]

We will discuss three cabinet-level departments here—Energy, Commerce, and Defense. As noted earlier, these departments were chosen because of the wealth of information each generates, distributes, and controls. The departments are presented as an example of government information—that which is restricted because of its being proprietary or personal data, or that which is classified due to the U.S. security regulations, as well as information that is unclassified.

It is impossible to look at each department and agency in depth here, but this sample should point out government sources of information and indicate the relationship between government and business, especially in the areas of aerospace research and defense. It is obviously not exhaustive.

Department of Energy

The Department of Energy (DOE) was established by the Department of Energy Organizational Act, August 4, 1977, pursuant to Executive Order 12009, September 13, 1977. It became effective October 1, 1977. DOE consolidated federal energy functions along with parts of the Departments of Interior, Commerce, Housing and Urban Development, Navy, and the Interstate Commerce Commission.

DOE provides the framework for a comprehensive and balanced national energy plan through the coordination and administration of the energy functions of the federal government. The department is responsible for long-term, high-risk research and development of energy technology; the marketing of federal power; energy conservation; nuclear weapons programs; energy regulatory programs; and a central energy data collection and analysis program.

DOE activities include nuclear energy, fossil energy, conservation and renewable energy, defense programs, environmental protection, safety, and emergency preparedness, energy research, and civilian radioactive waste management.

The work in these areas is carried out in government-owned facilities that are managed and administered by DOE Operations Offices in California, Idaho, Illinois, Nevada, New Mexico, South Carolina, Tennessee, and Washington. These facilities are referred to as Government-Owned Contractor-Operated (GOCO).

The Economic Regulatory Administration, Federal Energy Regulatory Commission (an independent organization within DOE), and Energy Information Administration are also a part of DOE's organizational structure. Of most interest here (although the others should not be ignored) is the data publication and distribution services provided by DOE—to other sections of DOE, to other parts of the government, and to the public. Included are the collecting, processing, and publication of data in the areas of energy resource reserves, energy production, demand, consumption, distribution, and technology. Analyses are prepared on energy data to assist government and nongovernment users in understanding energy trends; complex, long-term energy trends and the microeconomic and macroeconomic impacts of energy trends on regional and industrial sectors; and on competition within the energy industries, the capital and financial structure of energy companies, and interfuel substitutions. Audits are conducted to ensure the validity of regulatory and other energy data. For now it is sufficient to note that this is a cabinet-level department that generates not only unclassified data but also information that is restricted because of its relevance to national security and the U.S. economy.

Department of Commerce

The Departments of Commerce and Labor were reorganized under two Acts. The Act of February 14, 1903, pulled all labor activities together into the Department of Labor, and the Act of March 4, 1913, designated the Commerce Department.

The Department of Commerce (DOC) encourages, serves, and promotes the nation's international trade, economic growth, and technological advancement. Within this framework it promotes the national interest by encouraging the competitive free enterprise system. DOC offers assistance and information to help increase exports; administers programs to prevent unfair foreign trade competition; provides social and economic statistics and analyses for business and government planners; provides research and support for the increased use of scientific, engineering, and technological development; grants patents and registers trademarks; provides assistance to promote domestic economic development; seeks to improve understanding of the earth's physical environment and oceanic life; promotes travel to the United States by residents of foreign countries; and assists in the growth of minority businesses.

Commerce includes such organizations within its purview as National Oceanic and Atmospheric Administration (NOAA), National Bureau of Standards (NBS), Patents and Trademarks Office (PTO), Bureau of the Census, Bureau of Economic Analysis (BEA), Bureau of Industrial Economics, and International Trade Administration (ITA).

The mission of these Commerce Department facilities will be described to provide a view of a large body of mostly unclassified information generated by the U.S. government.

National Oceanic and Atmospheric Administration (NOAA)

This facility is set up to explore the global ocean and its living resources; to manage, use, and conserve those resources; and to describe, monitor, and predict conditions in the atmosphere, ocean, sun, and space environment. In addition NOAA issues warnings against impending destructive natural events, develops beneficial methods of environmental modification, and assesses the consequences of inadvertent environmental modification over time.

National Bureau of Standards (NBS)

The Bureau's goal is to strengthen and advance the nation's scientific technology and to facilitate its effective application for public benefit. To this end, NBS conducts research and provides a basis for the nation's physical measurement system, scientific and technological services for industry, ensuring U.S. involvement in domestic and international product standardization activities, maintaining equity in trade, and technical services promoting public safety.

Patents and Trademarks Office (PTO)

The PTO examines design patents (issued for fourteen years), plant patents (issued for seventeen years), and utility patents (issued for seventeen years). It also examines and issues patents and registers trademarks; sells copies of printed documents; records and indexes documents transferring ownership; and has a scientific library and search files containing over twenty-five million documents, including foreign patents. PTO provides search rooms for the public, handles appeals on inventions and trademarks, participates in legal proceedings and represents the U.S. in international efforts regarding patent and trademark policies.

Bureau of the Census

Established in 1902, the functions of the Bureau of the Census were provided for in the Constitution, which requires taking a census of population every ten years. The law (Title 13. U.S. Code) also provides that the information collected by the bureau from individual persons, households, or establishments be kept strictly confidential and be used only for statistical purposes.

The Bureau is a general purpose statistical agency which collects, tabulates, and publishes a wide variety of statistical data about the people and the economy of the nation. These data are utilized by the Congress, the executive branch, and the public generally in the development and evaluation of economic and social programs.

Bureau of Economic Analysis (BEA)

The BEA provides a picture of the U.S. economy through the preparation, development, and interpretation of the national income and products accounts, summarized by the gross national product (GNP); the wealth accounts, which show the business and other components of national wealth; the input-output accounts, which trace the interrelationships among industrial markets; personal income and related economic series by geographic area; the U.S. Balance of Payments accounts and associated foreign investment accounts; and measures relating to environmental change within the framework of the national economic accounts.

Bureau of Industrial Economics

This bureau provides government and business decision-makers with the data, research, and analytical support needed to assess the individual industry implications of major policy decisions and worldwide economic developments.

International Trade Administration (ITA)

Established in 1980, ITA promotes world trade and investments to strengthen the international trade and investment position of the United States.

Department of Commerce Services

Some of the services provided by the department are Environmental Data and Information Services, National Oceanographic Data, National Earth Satellite Service, National Ocean Survey, National Weather Service, National Geodetic Information Center, National Telecommunications and Information Administration (NTIA), and the National Technical Information Service (NTIS). NTIS is discussed in the next chapter, as a major distribution point for scientific and technical information.

Department of Defense

The Department of Defense (DOD) is the successor agency to the National Military Establishment created by the National Security Act of 1947. It was established as an executive department of the government by the National Security Act Amendments of 1949.

DOD is responsible for providing the military forces needed to deter war and protect the security of our country. The major elements of these forces are the Army, Navy, Marine Corps, and Air Force, consisting of about 2.1 million men and women on active duty. Of these, some 530,000—including about 75,000 on ships at sea—serve outside the United States. They are backed, in case of emergency, by the 2.3 million members of the reserve components. In addition, there are about one million civilian employees in the Defense Department.

Under the president, the Secretary of Defense exercises authority over the department, which includes the separately organized military departments of Army, Navy, and Air Force, the Joint Chiefs of Staff providing military advice, the unified and specified combatant commands, and various defense agencies established for specific purposes. Every state in the Union has some defense activities. Central headquarters of the department is at the Pentagon, the "world's largest office building."

DOD agencies include the Defense Communications Agency, Defense Nuclear Agency, Defense Mapping Agency, and the Defense Intelligence Agency, as well as others. However, within the department framework the most important center for the dissemination of defense information is the Defense Technical Information Center (DTIC). This will be discussed in detail in the next chapter.

INDEPENDENT AGENCIES

Besides the departments under the executive branch there are many important sources of information known as independent agencies, a group which has sometimes been called "the fourth branch of government." Table I (on pages 132–133) consists of a listing of several dozen agencies in this category. Listed below is a description of one of the most significant organizations in this category, an agency that is responsible for important work and which issues a large amount of technical data.

National Aeronautics and Space Administration

The National Aeronautics and Space Administration (NASA) was established by the National Aeronautics and Space Act of 1958.

NASA has the responsibility to conduct research for flight within and outside the earth's atmosphere and to develop, construct, test, and operate aeronautical and space vehicles. Furthermore it is charged with conducting research, with coordinating space research with other nations, and with disseminating information concerning its activities. It has five program offices, each responsible for some aspect of its overall program goals, and it also operates several field installations, where testing and research projects are performed.

SOURCES OF INFORMATION CONCERNING THE U.S. GOVERNMENT

It should be remembered that government departments go through reorganization just as commercial enterprises do, usually reflecting the current administration's thinking. The reporting and control structures change accordingly. Such changes can affect the access to and distribution of information; therefore it is important to know the official sources that reflect those changes.

The *Federal Register*[11] is one such source for government information. This daily publication includes presidential documents, regulatory documents with general applicability and legal effect, proposed rules, and documents that are published as required by statute. In addition, the *Code of Federal Regulations*,[12] the *Weekly Compilation of Presidential Documents*[13] and the *Public Papers of the Presidents*[14] are published as special editions of the *Federal Register*.

Other useful and informative publications of the Office of the Federal Register include the *United States Statutes at Large*[15] and the *Codification of Presidential Proclamations and Executive Orders*.[16] In addition, the Federal Information Center, operated by the General Services Administration, is designed to answer any questions about government programs, activities, or agencies. Directories for state, municipal, and county executives are also available.[17]

GOVERNMENT INFORMATION FROM THE PRIVATE SECTOR

Private business enterprises, universities, and not-for-profit research and development facilities should not be neglected as sources of government information. These organizations create a large percentage of the information which is controlled and distributed through government information centers. This is especially true in the subject fields related to aerospace research and defense. Generally these organizations remain active in this arena over long periods of time.[18]

Table III (pages 138–140) shows the top one hundred DOD contractors for 1983, in terms of net contract value. Table IV (pages 141–143) lists the top one hundred contractors for research, development, test and evaluation, both DOD and other agencies. As you compare these two tables, you will observe a great deal of duplication between them. Further, a comparison of compilations for past years also shows major duplication. Table V (pages 144–146) is a list of the National Aeronautics and Space Administration's (NASA) top one hundred contractors. Here, too, is overlap with Tables III and IV.

As can be seen from these data, by following relatively few of the total number of United States businesses, universities, and not-for-profit organizations it becomes easier to recognize where government information is generated outside the government complex.

STATE AND LOCAL GOVERNMENT

Many state publications have a counterpart in federal publications. These can include: state legislative information; administrative data, such as laws and statutes; special reports of commissions; decisions of the courts; and reports on projects or programs in the state. Other information may concern agriculture, geological surveys, or health reports, for example.

Weech[19] looks at the characteristics of state government publications and reviews state publications bibliography. The *Monthly Checklist of State Publications* by the Library of Congress is the most substantial tool on state publications. It should be noted, however, that it does not include all publications because not all state documents are sent to them for inclusion. Many states prepare lists of their own state publications, and most have passed state publication depository laws, similar to the federal publications depository law.

City and local government information is not controlled or collected as well as state government information. *Government Publications: Key Papers*[20] includes three articles that address the control and use of this information. More recently some attempt has been made to improve the situation, specifically with the publication of the reference tool *Municipal Government Reference Sources: Publications and Collections.*[21] Another boost has been given to the identification of local needs for information through the joint efforts of NCLIS and the Department of Agriculture. That work has been published in the *Joint Congressional Hearing on the Changing Needs of Rural America: the Role of Libraries and Information Technology.*[22]

Other sources of state and local information include census data collected by the Department of Commerce, Bureau of the Census, and commercially published state, municipal, and county directories.[23]

INTERNATIONAL AND FOREIGN INFORMATION

Information is increasingly recognized as an important national resource. Evans and Vambery state, "In the postwar era, the role of global and regional international governmental organizations increased tremendously, and their activities influence the political, social, and cultural status and development of each country and of all mankind."[24]

United Nations

The United Nations is made up of the General Assembly, the Security Council, the Economic and Social Council, the Trusteeship Council, the International Court of Justice, and the Secretariat. The General Assembly has seven committees that deal with questions on political and security matters; social, humanitarian, and cultural affairs; trusteeship; administrative and budgetary; and legal issues. The Security Council is concerned with international peace and security. The Economic and Social Council uses commissions and committees to accomplish its tasks which relate to information on statistics, population, human rights, the status of women, narcotic drugs, and international commodity trade. The Trusteeship Council oversees trust territories and the International Court of Justice is the principal judicial organ of the U.N.

Evans and Vambery list special bodies set up by the U.N. and intergovernmental specialized agencies.

1. U.N. Children's Fund

2. U.N. Conference of Trade and Development

3. U.N. Development Program

4. U.N. Institute for Training and Research

5. U.N. Research for Social Development

6. World Food Program

7. Office of the U.N. High Commissioner for Refugees

8. Permanent Central Narcotics Board

The Intergovernmental Specialized Agencies are:

1. Food and Agricultural Organization (FAO)

2. International Atomic Energy Agency (IAEA)

3. International Bank for Reconstruction and Development (IBRD)

4. International Development Association (IDA)

5. International Finance Corporation (IFC)

6. International Monetary Fund (IMF)

7. International Civil Aviation Organization (ICAO)

8. International Labor Organization (ILO)

9. Intergovernmental Maritime Consultative Organization (IMCO)

10. International Telecommunication Union (ITU)

11. U.N. Educational, Scientific and Cultural Organization (UNESCO)

12. Universal Postal Union (UPU)

13. World Health Organization (WHO)

14. World Meteorological Organization (WMO)

15. General Agreement on Tariffs and Trade (GATT)

A considerable amount of data is produced by these bodies and listed in the monthly issues of the *United Nations Documents Index.*

In addition, there are specialized organizations within the regions, noted earlier, that are sources of government information, such as the North Atlantic Treaty Organization (NATO) in Europe and the League of Arab States (LAS) in the Middle East.[25] A number of articles[26] can also be found on specific countries which discuss the availability of their government publications.

The issue of access and availability of information is a global one, with problems particular to each country in its efforts to produce or obtain information. The American Society for Information Science (ASIS) dealt specifically with this issue in their 1984 annual meeting,[27] with sessions on "Building Information Bridges: How Can the U.S. Information Community Respond to Information Needs and Challenges of the Third World?" and "Current and Future Information Programs and Activities in Different Countries around the Globe."

Furthermore, in order to improve global information transfer, continued support and involvement of the U.S. government is critical in such organizations as the Federation Internationale de Documentation (FID). This organization has some seventy countries as members and concentrates on promoting the transfer and use of information, which is crucial if we are to survive and prosper as one world.

Although we generally regard restricted information as that information relating to national security and thereby controlled by the National Security Act as classified information, it is obvious that a great deal of government information generated and collected may also be proprietary in nature or personal. When this is the case, it must be given its own kind of protection. Thus, each department or agency within the government must protect citizens against abuse of personal data that it collects and ensure that information collected for one reason is not used for another. The Privacy Act of 1974 was established for this reason. On the other hand, to operate as a democracy, citizens must have access to information they require in their daily lives—hence the need for the Freedom of Information Act and the Sunshine Act. It is also recognized that it is necessary to protect the U.S. economy and national security.

We need to remember that information is a global resource, and it must be made available in a reasonable manner and at a reasonable cost to the citizenry of the world. This becomes an even more important task for information professionals with increasing technology and information-based societies.

REFERENCES

1. Hoduski, Bernadine. *Policies and availability of government documents.* Arlington, VA: Committee on Information Hangups; 1984; July 18.

A talk presented on "Further Revisions to Printing and Binding Regulations of the Joint Committee on Printing."

2. McCallum, S.V. Legal research for non-law librarians. *Government Publications Review.* 6(3): 263–273; 1979.

Discusses legal research relating to reference questions asked in academic, public, and law libraries. Includes specific examples on legal citation forms and sample legal questions, as well as an excellent bibliography on legal sources.

3. Schwarzkopf, L. C. The Depository Library Program and access by the public to official publications of the United States Government. *Government Publications Review.* 5(2): 147–156; 1978.

Provides information on the programs for public access to government publications and information, a historical account, and issues and problems in the depository library system.

4. *United States Government Manual, 1984/85.* Washington: Office of the Federal Register; l984. 913p.

As the official handbook of the federal government, it provides comprehensive information on the agencies of the legislative, judicial, and executive branches. The *Manual* also includes information on quasi-official agencies, international organizations in which the United States participates, and boards, committees, and commissions.

The agency descriptions include a list of principal officials, a summary statement on the agency's purpose and role in the government, a brief history of the agency, including its legislative or executive authority, a description of its programs and activities, and a "Sources of Information" section. This last section provides information on consumer activities, contracts and grants, employment, publications, and many other areas of citizen interest.

5. *Federal Staff Directory, 1985.* Charles B. Brownson and Anna L. Brownson, Editor. Washington: Congressional Staff Directory, Ltd.; 1985. 1346p.

This publication lists information on the executive branch, 27,000 key executives, staff assistants and 1,500 staff biographies. It also includes an index by key word and individual. From this issue it is also possible to determine which of the nineteen largest departments and agencies have received the greater staff cuts, as well as staff gains, an indicator of current administration emphasis and funding. It is hoped that this feature will be continued.

6. *Federal Organization Service – Civil; Federal Organization Service – Military*. Washington: Carroll Publishing Co. Updated every 90 days.

This service includes charts of all cabinet-level departments, independent agencies, the Congress and the military services. Over 200 federal organization charts are included which show functional relationships of 18,000 individuals and contain names, titles, addresses, and room and telephone numbers. Charts cover 1,600 civil and 900 military departments, bureaus, and offices. These services include alphabetic and keyword functional indexes and includes custom research.

7. *Federal Executive Directory*. Washington: Carroll Publishing Company. Updated bimonthly.

Nearly 36,000 federal offices, including executive and congressional, are listed organizationally, and individuals are listed alphabetically. It also includes a keyword index and cross-references.

8. *Federal Regional Executive Directory*. Washington: Carroll Publishing Company. Updated twice a year.

Nearly 32,000 federal regional offices are listed, in addition to home-state offices of members of Congress, key personnel of federal District and Appeals Courts, and contacts for military bases. Executives are listed alphabetically, agencies are indexed by location (city and state), and subagencies are listed alphabetically.

9. Gamarekian, Barbara. Washington business: keeping track of the bureaucrats. *New York Times*. 1981 Jan. 4: Business Section.

This article describes some of the tools used for accessing government information and government employees.

10. *United States Government Manual*.

11. *Federal Register*. Washington: U.S. Office of the Federal Register.

Includes federal agency regulations and proposals for changes in regulated areas. This daily is published in an annual format entitled *Code of Federal Regulations*.

12. *Code of Federal Regulations.* Washington: U.S. Office of the Federal Register.

An annual codification of the general and permanent rules published in the *Federal Register.* The *Code* is divided into fifty titles that represent broad areas subject to federal regulations. The *Code* is kept up-to-date by the individual issues of the *Federal Register.*

13. *Weekly Compilation of Presidential Documents.* Washington: U.S. Office of the Federal Register.

Reference source for the public policies and activities of the president. It contains the remarks, news conferences, messages, statements, and other presidential material issued by the White House.

14. *Public Papers of the President.* Washington: U.S. Office of the Federal Register.

A companion publication to the *Weekly Compilation,* noted above, which provides public presidential documents and speeches in book form. This series begins with President Truman, but volumes covering the administration of President Hoover are also available.

15. *United States Statutes at Large.* Washington: U.S. Office of the Federal Register.

Slip laws, which are pamphlet prints, published by the U.S. Office of the Federal Register, of each public and private law enacted by Congress, are compiled annually for this publication. It also includes concurrent resolutions to these laws, enacted during a session of Congress, reorganization plans, proposed and ratified amendments to the Constitution, and presidential proclamations. Included in many of these documents are sidenotes, notations, and a guide to their legislative history.

16. *Codification of Presidential Proclamations and Executive Orders.* Washington: U.S. Office of the Federal Register.

This reference source is for proclamations and Executive Orders with general applicability and continuing legal effect. Its fifty chapters represent broad subject areas, as indicated also in the *Code of Federal Regulations.* Incorporated into each codified document are all amendments that were in effect on the most recent revision date.

17. *State, Municipal, and County Executive Directories.* Washington: Carroll Publishing Company. Updated two or three times a year, depending on the directory, and also available in combinations as annual publications.

The state publication includes executive branch and legislative officials of the fifty state governments. Executives of 1,200 municipalities with populations over 25,000 are listed with addresses, population size, county, state, and locator telephone number. Primary managers for 750 counties with populations of 50,000 or more are given with their names, addresses and telephone numbers. Each directory includes alphabetical listings and is cross-indexed to the organizational section.

18. *Defense Industry Organization Service.* Washington: Carroll Publishing Company.

Includes over 180 organizational charts of all major aerospace and electronic companies, as well as other firms, accounting for more than half of the total defense budget.

19. Weech, T. L. The characteristics of state government publications, 1910–1969. *Government Publications Review.* 1: 29–52; 1973.

This work was done to meet some of the requirements of a doctorate in library science. The analysis is based on Merritt's analysis of federal publications in 1943.

20. Fry, Bernard M.; Hernon, Peter. *Government publications: key papers.* (Guides to official publications; v.8) Elmsford, NY: Pergamon Press; 1981. 814p.

A collection of papers, previously published in professional journals, on topics of bibliographic control, acquisitions, classification, and cataloging of government publications.

21. American Library Association. Government Documents Round Table, et al., *Municipal government reference sources: publications and collections.* New York: R. R. Bowker Company; 1978. 341p.

Provides basic reference assistance in obtaining municipal government publications. It includes information on municipal publications, libraries, and databases for filling reference requests about local government activities and functions.

22. United States Department of Agriculture and the National Commission on Libraries and Information Science (NCLIS). *Joint congressional hearing on the changing information needs of rural America: the role of libraries and information technology.* July 21, 1982. Washington: GPO; SN 449 161 19025. 82p.

Includes testimony given at the hearing on rural information needs.

23. *State, Municipal and County Executive Directories.*

24. Evans, L. H.; Vambery, J. T. Documents and publication of contemporary international governmental organizations. *Law Library Journal.* 64: 338–362; 1971 Aug.

Lists international governmental organizations and describes their structure and notes problems involved in their publications. Includes a good reference list for further consultation for those interested in a more comprehensive look at dealing with international publications.

25. Ibid.

26. Fry.

27. *American Society for Information Science (ASIS). 47th Annual Meeting.* October 21–25, 1984. Philadelphia, Pa.

This conference had as its theme "1984: Challenges to an Information Society."

NOTE: The definitions and notes on the government publications referenced above are from the *United States Government Manual, 1983/84.*

TABLE I

INDEPENDENT ESTABLISHMENTS AND GOVERNMENT CORPORATIONS

ACTION
Administrative Conference of the United States
American Battle Monuments Commission
Appalachian Regional Commission
Board for International Broadcasting
Central Intelligence Agency
Civil Aeronautics Board
Commission on Civil Rights
Commission of Fine Arts
Commodity Futures Trading Commission
Consumer Product Safety Commission
Environmental Protection Agency
Equal Employment Opportunity Commission
Export-Import Bank of the United States
Farm Credit Administration
Federal Communications Commission
Federal Deposit Insurance Corporation
Federal Election Commission
Federal Emergency Management Agency
Federal Home Loan Bank Board
Federal Labor Relations Authority
Federal Maritime Commission
Federal Mediation and Conciliation Service
Federal Reserve System
Federal Trade Commission
General Services Administration
Inter-American Foundation
Interstate Commerce Commission
Merit Systems Protection Board
National Aeronautics and Space Administration
National Capital Planning Commission
National Credit Union Administration
National Foundation on the Arts and the Humanities
National Labor Relations Board
National Mediation Board
National Science Foundation

National Transportation Safety Board
Nuclear Regulatory Commission
Occupational Safety and Health Review Commission
Office of Personnel Management
Panama Canal Commission
Peace Corps
Pennsylvania Avenue Development Corporation
Pension Benefit Guaranty Corporation
Postal Rate Commission
Railroad Retirement Board
Securities and Exchange Commission
Selective Service System
Small Business Administration
Tennessee Valley Authority
United States Arms Control and Disarmament Agency
United States Information Agency
United States Information Development Cooperation Agency
United States International Trade Commission
United States Postal Service
Veterans Administration

NOTE: This information is from the *United States Government Manual*, 1984/85.

TABLE II

INDEPENDENT AGENCIES

ACTION
Administrative Conference of the United States
Advisory Commission on Intergovernmental Relations
Advisory Committee on Federal Pay
Agency for International Development (AID)
Alaska Natural Gas Transportation System
American Battle Monuments Commission
American Red Cross
Amtrak
Appalachian Regional Commission
Architectural and Transportation Barrier Compliance
    Board
Board of Governors of the Federal Reserve System
Board for International Broadcasting
Central Intelligence Agency
Civil Aeronautics Board
Commission on Bioethics
Commission on Civil Rights
Commission on Executive, Legislative and Judicial
    Salaries
Commission on Fine Arts
Committee for Purchase from the Blind
Commodity Futures Trading Commission
Congressional Budget Office
Consumer Product Safety Commission
Copyright Royalty Tribunal
Corporation for Public Broadcasting
Delaware River Basin Commission
Depository Institutions De-regulation Committee
Environmental Protection Agency
Equal Employment Opportunity Commission
Export-Import Bank of the United States
Farm Credit Administration
Federal Communications Commission
Federal Deposit Insurance Corporation
Federal Election Commission
Federal Emergency Management Agency

Federal Home Loan Bank Board
   Federal Home Mortgage Corporation
   Neighborhood Reinvestment Corporation
Federal Labor Relations Authority
Federal Maritime Commission
Federal Mediation and Conciliation Service
Federal Mine Safety and Health Review Commission
Federal National Mortgage Association
Federal Trade Commission
Foreign Trade Zones Board
General Accounting Office
General Services Administration
   Federal Information Centers
   Federal Supply and Services
   Federal Property Resources Service
   National Archives and Records Service
   Public Buildings Service
Gorgas Memorial Institute of Tropical and Preventive Medicine
Government Printing Office
Harry S. Truman Scholarship Foundation
Institute of Museum Services
Inter-American Foundation
International Bank for Reconstruction and Development (World
   Bank)
International Joint Commission, U.S. and Canada
Interstate Commerce Commission
Interstate Commission on the Potomac River Basin
John F. Kennedy Center for the Performing Arts
Legal Services Corporation
Library of Congress
Marine Mammal Commission
National Academy of Sciences
National Academy of Engineering
   Institute of Medicine
   National Research Council
National Aeronautics and Space Administration
National Capital Planning Commission
National Commission on Libraries and Information Science
National Consumer Cooperative Bank
National Council on the Handicapped
National Credit Union Administration
National Endowment for Democracy

National Foundation on the Arts and the Humanities
    National Endowment for the Arts
    National Endowment for the Humanities
National Gallery of Art
National Labor Relations Board
National Railroad Adjustment Board
National Mediation Board
National Science Foundation
National Transportation Safety Board
Nuclear Regulatory Commission
Occupational Safety and Health Review Commission
Office of Personnel Management
Overseas Private Investment Corporation
Panama Canal Commissions
Peace Corps
Pennsylvania Avenue Development Corporation
Pension Benefit Guaranty Corporation
Postal Rate Commission
Private Sector Survey on Cost Control
Railroad Retirement Board
Securities and Exchange Commission
Securities Investor Protection Corporation
Selective Service System
Small Business Administration
Smithsonian Institution
    Anacostia Neighborhood Museum
    Archives of American Art
    Cooper-Hewitt Museum of Design and Decorative Arts
    Freer Gallery of Art
    Hirshhorn Museum and Sculpture Garden
    National Air and Space Museum
    National Armed Forces Museum Advisory Board
    National Museum of African Art
    National Museum of American Art
    National Museum of American History
    National Museum of Natural History
    National Portrait Gallery
    National Zoological Park
    Smithsonian Astrophysical Observatory
    Smithsonian Environmental Research Center
    Smithsonian Marine Station at Link Port
    Smithsonian Tropical Research Institute

Student Loan Marketing Association
Susquehanna River Basin Commission
Synthetic Fuels Corporation
Tennessee Valley Authority
Trade and Development Program
U.S. Arms Control and Disarmament Agency
U.S. Holocaust Memorial Council
U.S. Information Agency
U.S. International Trade Commission
U.S. Merit Systems Protection Board
U.S.—Panama Joint Commission on the Environment
United States Postal Service
U.S. Railway Association
U.S. Soldiers' and Airmen's Home
Veterans Administration
Washington Metropolitan Area Transit Authority
Washington National Monument Society
Woodrow Wilson International Center for Scholars

NOTE: This information is from the *Federal Staff Directory*, 1985.

TABLE III

TOP 100 DEFENSE DEPARTMENT CONTRACTORS: FY 1984
(Net contract value in $ thousands)

1. *Boeing Company, Inc. – $1,788,529
2. *Lockheed Missiles and Space Company, Inc. – 1,156,553
3. *Rockwell International Corporation – 954,037
4. *General Electric – 848,238
5. *Martin Marietta Corporation – 813,576
6. *General Dynamics Corporation – 695,923
7. *McDonnell Douglas Corporation – 588,448
8. *Hughes Aircraft Company – 575,936
9. *Westinghouse Electric Corporation – 523,133
10. *TRW, Inc. – 455,373
11. *Sperry Corporation – 443,666
12. *Raytheon Company – 408,161
13. *IBM – 315,114
14. *Northrop Corporation – 297,422
15. *Aerospace Corporation – 273,409
16. *Johns Hopkins University – 272,814
17. Draper Charles Stark Lab – 267,178
18. Massachusetts Institute of Technology – 260,882
19. *United Technologies Corporation – 254,772
20. *Honeywell, Inc. – 246,249
21. *Mitre Corporation – 238,367
22. *Grumman Aerospace Corporation – 219,824
23. *RCA Corporation – 203,880
24. *Aerojet Strategic Propulsion Company – 196,699
25. *LTV Aerospace and Defense Company – 187,599
26. *Williams International Corporation – 178,015
27. *Ford Aerospace and Communications – 159,512
28. *GTE Products Corporation – 158,835
29. *GTE Service Corporation – 153,167
30. *AVCO Corporation – 140,741
31. *Texas Instruments, Inc. – 127,413
32. *Morton Thiokol, Inc. – 126,889
33. *Sanders Associates, Inc. – 112,494
34. *Interstate Electronics Corporation – 109,365
35. *ITT Corporation – 107,697
36. *Singer Company – 105,456

37. *Motorola, Inc. – 98,307
38. *Harris Corporation – 78,824
39. *Bell Helicopter/Textron – 77,330
40. *Lockheed Corporation – 76,380
41. *ESL, Inc. – 73,159
42.   Bell-Boeing JV – 72,849
43. *Fairchild Industries, Inc. – 72,806
44. *Science Applications Int. Corp. – 69,014
45. *Eaton Corporation – 63,507
46. *BDM Corporation – 63,295
47. *Calspan Corporation – 60,656
48. *Garrett Corporation – 57,044
49. *Logicon, Inc. – 52,564
50. *AT&T Technologies, Inc. – 51,571
51. *Teledyne, Inc. – 51,426
52. *Hercules, Inc. – 50,438
53. *Sverdrup Technology, Inc. – 48,606
54. *ITT Westinghouse JV – 48,582
55. *Computer Sciences Corporation – 45,665
56. *Magnavox – 45,197
57. *Litton Systems, Inc. – 44,700
58.   University of California – 44,631
59. *SRI International – 44,031
60.   Global Associates – 43,062
61. *Hazeltine Corporation – 42,504
62. *ITT Research Institute – 42,476
63.   Automation Industries – 41,517
64.   R&D Associates – 38,286
65.   University of Texas – 36,983
66.   AAI Corporation – 35,978
67. *System Development Corporation – 35,244
68. *Emerson Electric Company – 34,450
69. *Bendix Corporation – 31,342
70. *Textron, Inc. – 30,548
71. *Rand Corporation – 28,888
72.   Unidynamics Corporation – 28,597
73.   Stanford Leland University – 27,926
74.   Systems Research Laboratory – 27,068
75.   University of Southern California – 26,140
76.   Bolt Beranek & Newman, Inc. – 25,729
77. *Kaman Sciences Corporation – 25,462
78.   Georgia Tech Research Corp. – 25,378

79. *Norden Systems, Inc. – 24,168
80. Electrospace Systems, Inc. – 24,108
81. Institute for Defense Analyses – 23,629
82. *Goodyear Aerospace Corporation – 23,217
83. Hudson Institute – 22,839
84. *FMC Corporation – 22,583
85. *Battelle Memorial Institute – 22,388
86. *Control Data Corporation – 22,356
87. Atlantic Research Corporation – 21,404
88. Canadian Commercial Corporation – 20,608
89. University of New Mexico – 20,504
90. *Tracor, Inc. – 20,259
91. *Planning Research Corporation – 20,181
92. Solar Turbines, Inc. – 19,103
93. Pennsylvania State University – 18,913
94. University of Washington – 18,114
95. Itek Corporation – 17,993
96. Booz Allen & Hamilton – 17,750
97. Chrysler Corporation – 17,676
98. *Aerojet General Corporation – 17,408
99. Jaycor – 16,806
100. Amex Systems, Inc. – 16,795

---

*Companies listed in the *Defense Industry Organization Service.*

NOTE: Reprinted, with permission from the *Defense Industry Organization Service,* Carroll Publishing Co.

TABLE IV

TOP 100 CONTRACTORS FOR RESEARCH, DEVELOPMENT,
TEST AND EVALUATION FY 1983
(Net contract value in $ thousands)

1. *Boeing Company – $1,703,491
2. *Rockwell International Corporation – 1,171,720
3. *Martin Marietta Corporation – 1,048,660
4. *TRW Incorporated – 669,331
5. *McDonnell Douglas Corporation – 647,323
6. *General Electric Company – 645,426
7. *General Dynamics Corporation – 643,504
8. *Hughes Aircraft Company – 627,333
9. *Lockheed Missiles and Space Co., Inc. – 509,219
10. *United Technologies Corporation – 339,431
11. *International Business Machine Co. – 296,385
12. *Westinghouse Electronic Corporation – 293,277
13. *Raytheon Company – 266,373
14. *Aerospace Corporation – 260,474
15. Massachusetts Institute of Technology – 247,845
16. *Northrop Corporation – 245,512
17. *Johns Hopkins University – 226,703
18. *Honeywell Inc. – 218,371
19. *Vought Corporation – 210,841
20. *Mitre Corporation – 204,242
21. *Avco Corporation – 199,514
22. *Lockheed Corporation – 199,514
23. *GTE Products Corporation – 192,997
24. *Sperry Corporation – 182,690
25. *RCA Corporation – 181,732
26. *Morton Thiokol Incorporated – 147,735
27. *ITT Corporation – 146,981
28. *Grumman Aerospace Corporation – 131,781
29. *Aerojet Strategic Propulsion Company – 123,352
30. *Textron Incorporated – 116,426
31. *Singer Company – 110,583
32. *Aerojet General Corporation – 105,802
33. *Ford Aerospace and Communications – 98,343
34. *Hercules Incorporated – 94,862
35. *Harris Corporation – 91,514

36.   Automation Industries Incorporated – 88,049
37.   Charles Stark Draper Labs Inc. – 85,509
38.   *Science Applications Incorporated – 67,422
39.   *Motorola Incorporated – 64,297
40.   *Western Electric Company Inc. – 62,750
41.   *Calspan Corporation – 58,168
42.   Unidynamics St. Louis Incorporated – 57,433
43.   *Sanders Associates Incorporated – 56,726
44.   *Texas Instruments Incorporated – 53,927
45.   ITT and Westinghouse Joint Venture – 52,801
46.   *BDM Corporation – 49,631
47.   *Eaton Corporation – 49,305
48.   *Sverdrup Technology Incorporated – 45,849
49.   *SRI International – 43,685
50.   *Bendix Corporation – 42,120
51.   Illinois Institute Technology – 42,054
52.   *Computer Sciences Corporation – 42,238
53.   *Garrett Corporation – 41,081
54.   *University of California – 39,956
55.   *Litton Systems Incorporated – 38,986
56.   R&D Associates – 37,544
57.   *ESL Incorporated – 36,393
58.   TAD Communications Company – 36,268
59.   AAI Corporation – 34,707
60.   *Fairchild Industries Incorporated – 33,116
61.   *Emerson Electric Company – 31,287
62.   *E Systems Incorporated – 30,518
63.   *Teledyne Industries Incorporated – 28,318
64.   *Teledyne Brown Engineering – 28,301
65.   *Kentron International Incorporated – 27,549
66.   *FMC Corporated – 26,077
67.   Stanford University – 25,993
68.   *Hazeltine Corporation – 25,719
69.   *Logicon Incorporated – 25,255
70.   Georgia Technical Research Institute – 25,160
71.   *Rand Corporation – 23,811
72.   University of Texas – 23,250
73.   Bolt, Beranek and Newman Inc. – 22,797
74.   Institute for Defense Analyses – 22,440
75.   Systems Research Laboratories Inc. – 21,057
76.   *Battelle Memorial Institute – 20,667
77.   Pennsylvania State University – 20,436

78.   University of Rochester – 20,393
79.   *System Development Corporation – 20,342
80.   Western Gear Corporation – 20,091
81.   University of Southern California – 18,762
82.   *Planning Research Corporation – 18,674
83.   *Control Data Corporation – 18,552
84.   *Magnavox Govt. and Ind. Elect. Co. – 18,080
85.   *General Research Corporation – 16,990
86.   *AVCO Everett Research Laboratory – 16,861
87.   *Kaman Sciences Corporation – 16,615
88.   Atlantic Research Corporation – 15,508
89.   University of Washington – 15,269
90.   *Jaycor – 15,218
91.   Global Associates – 14,945
92.   University of Dayton – 14,809
93.   Booz Allen and Hamilton Incorporated – 14,623
94.   Amex Systems Incorporated – 14,231
95.   New Mexico State University – 14,013
96.   Electrospace Systems Incorporated – 13,505
97.   The Analytic Sciences Corporation – 13,447
98.   Sonicraft Incorporated – 13,363
99.   Hanson R A Company Incorporated – 13,294
100.*Boeing Vertol Company – 12,944

TOTAL $14,653,330

---

*Companies listed in the *Defense Industry Organization Service* totalling $13,580,778.

Defense Industry Organization Service includes:
· 69% of the top 100 companies
· 73% of total dollars
· 69 of 82 aerospace and electronics companies
· 98% of aerospace and electronics company dollars

Note: Reprinted with permission, from the *Defense Industry Organization Service*, Carroll Publishing Co.

TABLE V

TOP 100 NASA CONTRACTORS FY 1984
(Net contract value in $ thousands)

1.   *Rockwell International – $1,402,411
2.   *Martin Marietta – 427,788
3.   *Morton Thiokol, Inc. – 322,362
4.   *Lockheed Space – 301,357
5.   *General Dynamics – 252,515
6.   *McDonnell Douglas – 199,763
7.   *United Space Boosters – 196,520
8.   *Bendix Corp. – 162,643
9.   *International Business Machine – 134,408
10. *United Technologies – 117,924
11.   EG&G Florida Inc. – 109,357
12. *Ford Aerospace – 105,663
13. *Lockheed Engineering – 105,116
14. *Lockheed Missiles & Space – 102,096
15. *Computer Sciences Corp. – 89,465
16. *TRW Inc. – 82,291
17. *Perkin Elmer Corp. – 79,349
18. *RCA Corp. – 67,979
19. *Planning Research – 57,366
20. *Teledyne Industries – 51,528
21. *Boeing Co. – 44,188
22. *Singer Co. – 43,936
23. *General Electric – 43,553
24. *Hughes Aircraft – 42,163
25.   Pan American World Serv. – 40,296
26. *Ball Corp. – 39,088
27. *Northrop Services – 32,193
28. *Raytheon Service Co. – 27,764
29. *Westinghouse – 25,889
30. *Sperry Corp – 24,874
31. *Boeing Services Intl. – 24,797
32.   Air Products & Chemicals – 21,773
33.   Kentron International – 20,937
34. *Control Data Corp. – 20,221
35.   Management Tech. Services – 19,776
36. *Lockheed Corp. – 18,210

37. *Digital Equipment – 16,091
38. *Honeywell Inc. – 14,643
39. *System Development Corp. – 14,637
40. Bechtel National – 14,228
41. *Fairchild Industries – 13,553
42. Mechanical Technology – 12,972
43. *Grumman Aerospace – 12,559
44. Informatics General – 12,316
45. *Honeywell Info. Systems – 12,013
46. *Northrop Worldwide Acft. – 11,906
47. Sauer Mechanical – 11,768
48. Space Communications – 11,614
49. RMS Technologies – 11,427
50. Klate Holt Co. – 10,842
51. Garrett Corp. – 10,255
52. VEPCO – 10,003
53. *General Motors – 9,955
54. Technology Devel. – 9,889
55. ILC Industries – 9,858
56. Mercury Consolidated – 9,715
57. Wyle Laboratories – 9,103
58. *GTE Communication – 8,707
59. Analex Corp. – 8,665
60. Cleveland Electric – 8,279
61. Bionetics Corp. – 7,917
62. Cray Research Inc. – 7,753
63. *Sverdrup Technology – 7,700
64. C&P Telephone – 7,637
65. *AT&T – 7,566
66. Omniplan Corp. – 7,170
67. Specialty Maintenance – 7,167
68. *LTV Aerospace – 7,145
69. OAO Corp. – 7,008
70. *Fairchild Weston – 6,886
71. Management Services – 6,667
72. SYRE JV – 6,582
73. BAMSI Inc. – 6,421
74. *Harris Corp. – 6,205
75. *Science Appl. Res. JV – 6,188
76. Systems & Applied Science – 6,165
77. Sigma Data Services – 6,039
78. Smith Engineering – 5,885

79. *Motorola, Inc. – 5,621
80. PEPCO – 5,579
81. Amdahl Corp. – 5,369
82. Hudgins Construction – 5,316
83. Alpha Building – 5,312
84. Modular Computer – 5,069
85. Reynolds Smith & Hills – 5,024
86. Barrios Technology Inc. – 4,997
87. New Technology Inc. – 4,934
88. WLT Corp. – 4,922
89. Vion Corp. – 4,808
90. *Science Sys. Applications – 4,739
91. Intergraph Corp. – 4,719
92. Taft Broadcasting Corp. – 4,680
93. DEI East Inc. – 4,307
94. *Xerox Corp. – 4,304
95. Inter Con Security – 4,282
96. Johnson Engineering – 4,274
97. Datacom Inc. – 4,242
98. *IT&T – 4,241
99. Santa Barbara Research – 4,228
100.*Data General Corp. – 4,162

TOTAL $5,361,787

-----

*Companies listed in the *Defense Industry Organization Service.*

NOTE: Reprinted, with permission, from the *Defense Industry Organization Service,* Carroll Publishing Co.

Chapter Ten

Accessing and Obtaining
Government Information

FREEDOM OF INFORMATION ACT

The Freedom of Information Act (FOIA) was enacted in 1966 and revised in 1974. It allows access to official records and archival material as well as official publications which have been withheld from the public. The FOIA provides individuals with the opportunity to become better informed about government practices. The use of such statutes collectively ensures a more open form of government, based on democratic principles.

Numerous articles, books, and guides to the FOIA have been written. Briefly we will look at how to use this law and point to some specific issues regarding the FOIA and government information in general.

There are three very useful publications on the FOIA available for a small fee. The first is a simple brochure called *The Freedom of Information Act: What It Is and How to Use It*,[1] available from the Freedom of Information Clearinghouse, Box 19367, Washington, DC 20036. The brochure contains a general discussion on the types of information stored by the federal government, such as the safety performance of airlines and nutritional content of processed food, tests on consumer products, defense, foreign policy, and safety of nuclear generators, to name a few. It explains how to make a request, with sample letters, and discusses going to court to force delivery of wanted data. Furthermore, it offers the requester guidelines to judge reasonably if the agency is trying to avoid disclosing requested information, and gives exemptions of the FOIA. The clearinghouse is a project of Ralph Nader's Center for Study of Responsive Law and is supported entirely by contributions.

The second source is *A Citizen's Guide on How to Use the Freedom of Information Act in Requesting Government Documents*.[2] This Government Printing Office (GPO) publication is prepared by the House Committee on Government Operations and is a report from its Government Information and Individual Rights Subcommittee.

The third publication is also available from the GPO and is a *Freedom of Information Case List*,[3] by the Office of Information and Privacy, U.S. Department of Justice. This is a compilation of judicial decisions relating to the FOIA, the Privacy Act, the Sunshine Act, and the Federal Advisory Committee Act. It also includes reverse FOIA cases, a list of law review articles, and a "Short Guide to the Freedom of Information Act," which includes the citation of cases.

How to Use the FOIA

Using the FOIA is really very easy; in some cases a request for information may be in the form of a telephone call to the agency. If such an informal request is not sufficient, however, a letter of request is all that is necessary. The letter should be addressed to the Freedom of Information Unit and the name and address of the government agency. You can specify that your letter is a Freedom of Information Request in a subject or attention line. The body should cite the Freedom of Information Act, as 5 U.S.C. 552 and then state your request by describing the information you want, if the title of the publication is unknown to you. There can be search and copy fees that apply to your request but these are nominal, and if they seem excessive they should be questioned. Only direct costs for searching and copying may be charged under the FOIA. If you are asking for copies, then specify a maximum amount that you will pay, otherwise ask to be notified of the costs. Be sure to include your name and full address for their mailing. It is a good idea to identify the outside of the envelope as a FOIA request as well. In any appeal or follow-up letters, refer to your previous correspondence by date and use the same description as you used to describe the information requested in your first FOIA letter. Again, identify the request as being made under the FOIA in the body of the follow-up letter and on the outside of the envelope.

Some fees for FOIA requests are waived, for example in the case of writers for the press, scholars, authors, and researchers. In addition, you might choose to visit an agency to look at data there instead of getting reproductions. This is also permitted under the FOIA and will allow you to determine in advance how much information you require and get only the copies needed.

Should your FOIA request fail, you may sue in the United States District Court, where you live, where the documents are located, or in the District of Columbia, as you choose. There may be some costs involved. If you win, however, the court may require the government to pay your attorney's fees.

There are nine exemptions to the FOIA. These include information in the areas of: national defense and foreign policy; internal personnel rules and practices; information exempt under other rules; confidential business information; executive privilege; personal privacy; investigatory files; financial institution reports—regulatory agencies; and geological and geophysical information and data. The FOIA pertains only to access to federal government information; however, several states have their own freedom of information laws.

FOIA and Specific Information

Not all government agencies are content with the FOIA. Mitchell[4] gives an excellent history of classified information and historical research, including a discussion of the changes involved in handling that reflect the views of the president in office. He relates these historical events to the FOIA and its rise and decline, use, and interpretation, from Franklin Delano Roosevelt to the Reagan administration. He maintains that there is a necessity for historical research to include the secret dimension that exists in every U.S. government activity, if historical research is to be accurate and useful.

The Federal Bureau of Investigation (FBI) and the Central Intelligence Agency (CIA) continue to propose that their files be exempted under the FOIA.[5] Since the FOIA already exempts files that could adversely affect national security and foreign policy, it would seem that further exemption is unnecessary.

The current Presidential Executive Order 12356[6] removed existing downgrading and declassification schedules, allowing documents to be classified indefinitely. Generally, the policy now is closer to what it was in 1953 under Executive Order 10501. Furthermore, unclassified information requested under FOIA can be subsequently classified, requiring the requester to expend time and money if he or she wishes to challenge the legitimacy of the classification. In addition, the sixty-day limit for responding to a request was extended to one year.

Government information belongs to the people, and it is necessary for the citizen and the information professional to exercise their rights of access in order to preserve them. Restriction on information does not necessarily mean that it cannot be obtained. The FOIA is the statute that should be used to challenge that restriction so that the users' informational requirements are better served.

PRIVACY ACT

The Privacy Act of 1974 allows an individual to determine what records pertaining to him or her have been collected, maintained, used, or disseminated by federal agencies and to gain access to those records.

Like the FOIA, the Privacy Act has also had a lot of attention in the literature in general. The same guide[7] available from the GPO on the FOIA also explains how to use the Privacy Act in requesting government data. Where the FOIA provides access to information concerning the government, the Privacy Act is intended to assist individuals in obtaining information about themselves. Besides requiring the government to release your personal information to you from government files, the Privacy Act also requires the government to protect personal information from misuse and unauthorized disclosure. The *Case List*,[8] also referred to earlier, lists Privacy Act cases.

U.S. Government and Personal Data

The federal government has a vast amount of information concerning individuals. These records may include files on you if you have worked for a federal agency, worked as a government contractor, or been in the armed services. Information on you may be collected if you have participated in a federally financed project; arrest records, if fingerprints are taken, may be in FBI files; government subsidy records at the Department of Agriculture may exist on you; information on veterans benefits at the Veterans Administration is on file; student loan or grant information is collected in the Department of Education; security information for a clearance at the Department of Defense is available; and information on you may exist as a recipient of Medicare and Social Security benefits at the Department of Health and Human Services.

How to Use the Privacy Act

To tell where this information exists, the government agencies are required to publish annually in the *Federal Register* the existence and characteristics of all record systems and to identify those files that are exempted. To obtain information from these files, simply follow the same guidelines given above for the FOIA, referring to 5 U.S.C. 522a in any correspondence. Fees may also apply, and if your request is not satisfied you can take court action.

There are seven categories of exemption under the Privacy Act. These include the areas of:

1. Certain CIA and criminal law enforcement agencies' files;

2. National defense and foreign policy;

3. Investigatory files compiled for law enforcement;

4. Secret Service intelligence files;

5. Certain records used only for statistical purposes;

6. Investigatory material used for government employment, military service, federal contracts, and security clearances;

7. Evaluation material relating to decision-making and promotions in the armed services.

The CIA, along with the FBI, continues to request further exemptions of their files.[9] However, you should ask for anything you choose from any agency, since the burden is on the agency to prove that the exemption is justified. Furthermore, the agencies do not always use the exemptions they claim. In addition, you may also request that your records be amended, the *Citizen's Guide*[10] gives examples of correspondence to do this. There is no limit on response time under the Privacy Act as there is under the FOIA, so it might prove beneficial to invoke both acts in your request.

Other Personal Data

The issue of privacy is not limited to what the government collects but includes as well data provided voluntarily by people in their everyday lives. Recently the U.S. government has begun to obtain this data and to use it along with the data they are required to collect to carry out the business of the people. For example, mailing lists obtained from the private sector by the Internal Revenue Service

(IRS) are being used to determine if citizens are spending more income than they make. The theory is that through computer matching the IRS can identify people who are evading taxes.

This issue is in need of immediate attention in the United States to stem the tide of invasion of privacy by the government. The *Privacy Journal* regularly addresses these issues. However, other countries are far ahead of the U.S. in their development of comprehensive policies to protect the privacy of their citizens. Many European countries have established Data Protection Commissions as a result of new laws for protecting personal data. The annual meeting of the American Society for Information Science (ASIS) held special sessions on this topic in 1984.[11] These issues need to be, and likely will be, discussed more extensively here and abroad in view of the amount of personal data collected and manipulated by computer technology.

SUNSHINE ACT

The Sunshine Act directs that meetings of federal agencies headed by a collegial body composed of two or more individual members be open to the public. Mostly these include independent agencies that are regulatory commissions. This Act was another part of the open government movement which began in the 1960s and 1970s to alter perceptibly what information held by the government should be secret and what should be more open to the people. Previously the government had only one law for open meetings, the Federal Advisory Committee Act (FACA). Hartle and Chitwood[12] in a recent article looked at the success of the Sunshine Act in opening meetings, what influenced its implementation and its impact on the agencies it covers. They found both positive and negative aspects but the benefits outweighed detrimental effects. There is concern, however, over lack of oversight of the law or external review of transcripts of meetings to determine if closed meetings were justified.

If the 1960s and 1970s were an opening of our government, the 1980s could be termed a closing. It appears that this is not just President Reagan and his supporters in Washington. Hartle and Chitwood claim that our open government policy is precarious. They quote House Speaker Thomas P. "Tip" O'Neill, Jr., whose comments indicate the general feeling that Congress has gone too far in opening up sources of information and that public access has hurt the government's ability to function.

There is a delicate balance involved in achieving the right amount of secrecy and openness for both the government and the people. It is the duty of the citizen, and most especially the information professional, to help achieve this balance through open and active participation in the formulation of policy and law.

CONVENTIONAL SOURCES FOR OBTAINING GOVERNMENT INFORMATION

There is, certainly, an abundance of government information, as has been discussed. Some of this information is stored data, other is in the form of journals, reports of all kinds, and databases. It can be free or available for a nominal cost. It comes in different formats and can be distributed to restricted classes of users or be available to the general public and the world.

Here let us discuss some of the sources for obtaining government information. These include the Government Printing Office (GPO), Department of Energy Technical Information Center (DOE/TIC), National Technical Information Service (NTIS), Educational Resources Information Center (ERIC), Defense Technical Information Center (DTIC), and the National Aeronautics and Space Administration (NASA). There are specific reference tools[13],[14] that can help to identify additional sources to use in acquiring government information. In addition articles can be found that discuss some special issues related to the acquisition of technical reports.[15]

Government Printing Office

The Government Printing Office (GPO) provides publications and reports published by the executive, legislative, and judicial branches of the federal government. The Superintendent of Documents is also required to announce, distribute, and sell documents of general public interest. The Depository Library Program, discussed in Chapter 2, has an integral part in making this type of government information available. In addition GPO publishes on a subscription basis the *Monthly Catalog of United States Government Publications*. The *Catalog* lists government publications printed and processed by GPO and is available for online searching through BRS, DIALOG, and ORBIT. GPO handles some DOD pamphlets, manuals, and standards, and most prices for these and other documents are nominal, although there has been a recent trend toward higher prices.

Some out-of-print GPO publications can be obtained from NTIS as well as from one of the depository libraries. A list of depository libraries and GPO bookstores is available to assist in retrieval of government publications. Inquiries and requests may be addressed to Superintendent of Documents, Government Printing Office, North Capitol and H Streets, N.W., Washington, DC 20402.

Department of Energy Technical Information Center

The Department of Energy (DOE) is involved in nuclear energy, fossil energy, conservation and renewable energy, defense programs, environmental protection, safety and emergency preparedness, energy research, and civilian radioactive waste management. Because of this breadth of interests, a great deal of energy-related information is generated and is included in DOE's RECON system. This online retrieval system has one million references to energy-related information from books, journals, reports, patents, and conference proceedings, which are available to DOE and its contractors. Much of the information is unclassified and available also to the general public through DOE's Technical Information Center (DOE/TIC). Prices for reports are based on the number of pages to be copied, either on paper or on microfiche. DOE/TIC has a selected microfiche distribution program. DOE/RECON has online connect and print charges. Some energy reports are available through the GPO and NTIS. In addition, the classified portion of this data is available through DTIC. The regulations and laws concerning classification and access to DOE classified information is discussed in earlier chapters of this book. Inquiries and report requests may be addressed to the DOE Technical Information Center, Box 62, Oak Ridge, TN 37830.

National Technical Information Service

The National Technical Information Service (NTIS), part of the Department of Commerce, is the central source for the public sale of U.S. government and government-sponsored research, development, and engineering reports, as well as foreign technical reports and other analyses prepared by national and local government agencies, their contractors, or grantees. It is the central source for federally generated machine-processable data files, and it also manages the Federal Software Center for intragovernmental distribution. NTIS is one of the world's leading processors of specialty information, all of which is unclassified. NTIS publishes *Government Reports Announce-*

ments and Index, available on a subscription basis. Its bibliographic reference files are also available online through commercial vendors such as BRS, DIALOG, and ORBIT. Also available is SRIM/Profile, a program of automatic distribution of microfiche copies of documents tailored to the customer's subject profile. Prices for reports are based on a minimum charge plus the number of pages to be copied and whether a paper copy or microfiche is requested. Inquiries and technical report requests may be addressed to NTIS, 5285 Port Royal Road, Springfield, VA 22161.

Educational Resources Information Center

The Educational Resources Information Center (ERIC) is a decentralized nationwide network of sixteen subject-oriented clearinghouses. These clearinghouses publish bibliographies, reviews, and state-of-the-art studies that are indexed in *Resources in Education* (RIE), available on a subscription basis through GPO. The ERIC database is accessible through DIALOG, BRS, and ORBIT. Publications are available in paper copy or microfiche and price depends on format and number of pages copied. The online service has the usual usage fees associated with it. There are several libraries around the country which serve as depository agencies for ERIC reports, freely available to the public. Inquiries and requests should be addressed to ERIC, National Institute of Education, Washington, DC 20208.

Defense Technical Information Center

The Defense Technical Information Center (DTIC), formerly the Defense Documentation Center (DDC), organizationally comes under the Secretary of Defense, Assistant for Manpower, Installations and Logistics, Defense Logistics Agency (DLA). It is a component of the DOD scientific and technical information program. As such it provides access to and transfer of scientific and technical information for DOD personnel, DOD contractors and potential contractors, and other U.S. government agency personnel and their contractors. The unclassified portion of DTIC's technical reports are released through NTIS, however, they are also available through DTIC by registered users that have DOD contracts or qualify as potential contractors. (See the chapters on Military Information.)

Besides the 1.2 million technical reports under computer control, and an additional 300,000 available for manual searching, DTIC has four databases available to their registered users. These can be accessed through the Defense RDT&E On-line System (DROLS). The databases include: Research and Development Program Planning Data Base (R&DPP); Research and Technology Work Unit Information System (WUIS); Technical Reports (TR) database; and Independent Research and Development (R&D) database. Any government contractor may use the unclassified database, which also gives access to unclassified citations for classified reports. To get classified information on classified reports (i.e., classified searches online), you must have a cryptographic terminal. However, classified searches may be requested from DTIC and sent to contractor organizations.

DTIC also offers other services:

1. Automatic Document Distribution (ADD) program;

2. Automatic Magnetic Tape Dissemination (AMTD) program;

3. DTIC Current Awareness Bibliographies (CAB);

4. DTIC Referral Data Bank;

5. Information Analysis Centers (IAC);

6. DTIC Online Service Facilities.

In addition, DTIC publishes the *Technical Abstracts Bulletin* and the *Technical Abstracts Index* (now classified Confidential) available as a subscription. This publication lists DTIC reports, both classified and unclassified; however, like the other products and services, it is available only to registered users. Unclassified reports can be obtained through NTIS.

Both DTIC and NTIS offer paper copies or microfiche copies of these technical reports. DTIC has one price for paper copy and one price for microfiche. Recently, the minimum price for paper copy reports from DTIC were increased and now include a per page charge. Reports may be ordered online or by mail using DTIC order forms. Inquiries and requests should be addressed to DTIC, Building 5, Cameron Station, Alexandria, VA 22214.

National Aeronautics and Space Administration

The National Aeronautics and Space Administration (NASA) has a large program of research and development, which creates many technical reports, including a sizable number of translations of foreign publications. Many of the publications prepared by NASA or its contractors are available from NTIS. Those not available from NTIS may be obtained from information centers operated by the various NASA offices and field installations. In addition a reading room is maintained by NASA at its headquarters in Washington.

NASA sponsors two important indexing and abstracting services. One, known as *Scientific and Technical Aerospace Reports (STAR)*, deals only with technical reports. The other, *International Aerospace Abstracts*, covers mostly journal articles and conference papers.

STATE AND LOCAL GOVERNMENT

Earlier mention was made concerning the availability of state and local information from the Bureau of the Census. Such data can assist local and regional planning, for example. Other government agencies often collect and report statistical data by state or Standard Metropolitan Region (SMR). Leads to some of these sources may be found by looking at appropriate tables in the *Statistical Abstract of the U.S.*, each of which cites the agency from which the data was procured. Directories that list executive branch officials of the state governments, executives of municipalities and primary managers of counties in the United States and county government executives are available.[16] In addition several states have enacted their own freedom of information, privacy, and sunshine laws to allow for a more open state and local government. More information on this type of local activity is available from the Freedom of Information Clearinghouse, Box 19367, Washington, DC 20036, including the publication of a model state freedom of information statute and a list of states that have their own freedom of information laws—with references cited.

Many states have depository library legislation for state publications which requires, among other things, the deposit of a minimum number of copies of publications in the state library or in other libraries in the state. Lane's handbook[17] is an excellent source for pursuing this area of government information. Besides including characteristics of depository library legislation and what the literature has to contribute to our understanding of state publications, she also includes specifics on individual states and a "Model Law" for states that provide the Library of Congress with copies of their official publications. For help in accessing local publications the *Municipal*

Government Reference Sources: Publications and Collections is an excellent reference tool.[18]

INTERNATIONAL AND FOREIGN INFORMATION

In Chapter 9 we discussed international and foreign government information. References were suggested to learn more about foreign government information, such as articles on the British Lending Library and Her Majesty's Stationery Office (HMSO) publications. Here we will look at the acquisition of international information as it relates to the discussion in the previous chapter.

The United Nations serves as the single most important body for international government information. As noted earlier, a great deal of information is generated by the different specialized agencies. This information is available from different sources which are discussed in the following paragraphs.

United Nations Publications

The annual checklist of *United Nations Publications in Print* lists those titles available, usually in paper copy, and the language of each publication is noted in the sales number. Prices are in U.S. dollars. Other catalogs of U.N. publications include Standing Order Service, Microfiche Price List, U.N. Periodicals, U.N. Official Records, and International Court of Justice. Publications out of print may be available from other sources, including United Nations depository libraries. The Dag Hammarskjold Library, United Nations, New York,[19] administers a depository program for 327 libraries worldwide. Inquiries and requests for United Nations publications may be sent to United Nations Publications, Room A-3315, New York, NY 10017 or United Nations Publications, Palais des Nations, CH-1211 Geneva 10, Switzerland.

UNESCO

The United Nations Educational, Scientific, and Cultural Organization (UNESCO) has as its noble objective to contribute to peace and security. This organization publishes books and periodicals in such fields as education, science, social science, communications, and culture. UNESCO has 112 national distributors located around the world. Requests and inquiries may be addressed to UNESCO, Publishing Services, 7 Place de Fontenoy, 75700 Paris, France.

Unipub

At one time Unipub distributed publications only for the United Nations. It currently supplies United Nations publications as well as publications of some twenty-five other international agencies. Unipub publishes the *International Bibliography, Information, Documentation* (IBID), an annotated quarterly journal. Unipub will supply one-time orders as well as handle automatic shipment of materials in your selected categories. This may include monographs, technical reports, manuals, conference proceedings, statistical works, maps, periodicals, filmstrips, recordings, slides, microforms, and other documentation. The subjects covered include agriculture, alternative energy resources, arts and humanities, business and trade, communication, copyright, earth science, economics and development, education, ethnic studies, energy resources, engineering and technology, environment, food and nutrition, health services, labor relations, law, library and information science, life science, marine science and fisheries, meteorology, nuclear medicine, nuclear science, oceanography, population and demography, scientific maps and atlases, social and political science, and solar energy. Inquiries and requests may be addressed to Unipub, 345 Park Avenue South, New York, NY 10010.

Other Sources

Specific articles, not cited here, discuss foreign government information and its availability in such countries as Australia, Britain, and Canada, and others on the United Nations and other international organizations.[20] Specific sources for global regional organizations include the following, summarized from Evans and Vambery.[21]

Western Europe

Council of Europe (CE)

North Atlantic Treaty Organization (NATO)

Western European Union (WEU)

Benelux Economic Union (BEU)

Nordic Council (NC)

Organization for Economic Cooperation and Development (OECD)

European Coal and Steel Community (ECSC)

European Economic Community (EEC)

European Atomic Energy Community (EURATOM)

Eastern Europe

Communist Information Bureau (COMINFORM)

Warsaw Treaty Organization (WTO)

Council for Mutual Economic Aid (COMECON)

The Americas

Organization of American States (OAS)

Organization of Central American States (OCAS)

Central American Common Market (CACM)

Latin American Free Trade Association (LAFTA)

Middle East

League of Arab States (LAS)

Central Treaty Organization (CENTO)

Asia and the Far East

South Pacific Commission (SPC)

Colombo Plan (CP)

ANZUS Council

South-East Asia Treaty Organization (SEATO)

Africa

Organization of African Unity (OAU)

While these organizations unite countries in regional areas, at least on some basis, there are similar issues, relative to information and its access, confronting individual countries. Last year a special issue was published by *Government Publications Review;*[22] the topic was *Freedom of Information Developments Around the World: A Symposium.* It included articles on the Nordic countries, France, the United States, Sweden, Australia, the United Kingdom and Japan and a comparative perspective. Reynolds[23] in "Bibliographic Guide to Issues of National and International Government Information Policies" identifies additional references on foreign and international government information.

MICROFICHE COPIES OF DOCUMENTS

The reader should be aware that some commercial sources which index government publications also offer for sale microfiche copies of each item indexed, thus simplifying and speeding up access to such documents. One source, *State Publications Index*[24] is, as the title indicates, restricted to documents at the state level of government. At the urban and county level, the best source is *Index to Current Urban Documents.*[25]

At the federal level, a useful source of House and Senate documents available on microfiche is the *CIS/Index to Publications of the United States Congress.*[26] It is particularly strong in its handling of Congressional hearings.

REFERENCES

1. *Freedom of Information Act: what it is and how to use it.* Washington: Freedom of Information Clearinghouse.

A leaflet available from the Freedom of Information Clearinghouse, Box 19367, Washington, DC 20036. These are available in quantities for 10 cents each and would be useful for further distribution by library and information centers.

2. U.S. House Committee on Government Operations. *A citizen's guide on*

how to use the Freedom of Information Act and the Privacy Act in requesting government documents. Washington: GPO; 1977; SN 052 071 00540.4. 59p.

Covers the FOIA and the Privacy Act, discusses which act to use and how to request government documents and personal records.

3. U.S. Department of Justice, Office of Information and Privacy. *Freedom of Information case list.* Washington: 297p. GPO; 1983 Sept. 13.

Includes judicial decisions relating to the FOIA, the Privacy Act, the Sunshine Act and the Federal Advisory Committee Act, and other sections particularly useful to the researcher or lawyer.

4. Mitchell, Steven. Classified information and historical research. *Government Publications Review.* 10: 427–440; 1983.

Looks at the historical development of the United States security classification and procedures and how it relates to the FOIA. Executive Order 12356 is seen as a reversal of the progress made under two previous administrations.

5. Theoharis, Athan G. The Freedom of Information Act and the intelligence agencies. *Government Publications Review.* 9: 37–44; 1982.

The author objects to the FBI and CIA claims for exempting their agencies' files. He further questions their separate filing and compartmentalized record policies.

6. Executive Order 12356. *Federal Register.* 47(66): 14874–14884; 1982 April 6.

This Order on National Security Information was signed by President Reagan. It reverses the past two administrations in its handling of information and national security and is reminiscent of 1953, Executive Order 10501.

7. U.S. House Committee. *Citizen's guide.*

8. U.S. Department of Justice. *Case List.*

9. Theoharis.

10. U.S. House Committee. *Citizen's guide.*

11. *American Society for Information Science (ASIS). 47th Annual Meeting.* October 21–25, 1984, Philadelphia, PA.

Robert E. Smith, publisher of *Privacy Journal,* Washington, DC, spoke on

"The Challenge in the Information Age," relative to privacy of personal data. Michael E. D. Koenig moderated a panel discussion on internalization of information systems and services, including transborder data flow, cultural integrity, non-tariff trade barriers, privatization, and reciprocity of privacy legislation.

12. Hartle, Terry W.; Chitwood, Stephen R. Increasing public access to government; the implementation and impact of the government in the Sunshine Act. *Government Publications Review*. 10(3): 269–283; 1983 May–June.

This analysis of the Sunshine Act was based on data from statutorily mandated oversight reports during the first three years of the law and case studies of seven agencies.

13. Institute for Defense Analyses. *How to get it: a guide to defense-related information resources*. Washington: NTIS; 1982 Jan.; AD-A110-000; IDA Paper P-1500 (Rev.). 531p.

Useful for identifying and acquiring government published or government sponsored documents, maps, patents, specifications or standards, and other resources.

14. Global Engineering Documentation Service. *Directory of engineering document sources*. 3d. ed. 2625 Hickory Ave., Santa Ana, CA: Global; 1985. 700p.

Includes over 8,000 series of engineering, scientific, and management publications. This tool gives the document series name, the originating organizations, where that particular type of document is indexed, and the source of the document.

15. Newman, Wilda B. Acquiring technical reports in the special library: another package for information transfer. *Science & Technology Libraries*. 2(4): 45–67; 1982 Summer.

Discusses the importance of technical reports, their processing and maintenance, availability, current technology, and trends in document delivery.

16. *State, Municipal and County Executive Directories*. Washington: Carroll Publishing Company.

Updated two or three times a year, depending on the directory. Also available in combinations as annual publications.

The state publication includes executive branch and legislative officials of the 50 state governments. Executives of 1,200 municipalities with populations over 25,000 are listed with addresses, population size, county, state, and locator telephone number. Primary managers from 750 counties with populations of 50,000 or more are given with their names, addresses, and telephone numbers. Each directory includes alphabetical listings and is cross-indexed to the organizational section.

17. Lane, Margaret T. *State publications and depository libraries: a reference handbook.* Westport, CT: Greenwood Press; 1981. 573p.

Pulls together current state publication depository legislation and deals with the characteristics of the laws, current professional literature, and specific information on the individual states.

18. American Library Association. Government Documents Round Table, et al., *Municipal government reference sources: publications and collections.* New York: Bowker; 1978. 341p.

Provides basic reference assistance in obtaining a valuable information resource—municipal government publications. It includes information on municipal publications, libraries, and databases for filling reference requests about local government activities and functions.

19. Orlov, Vladimir. Serving the United Nations: the Dag Hammarskjold Library. *Wilson Library Bulletin.* 57: 640–645; 1983 April.

Discusses the United Nations library in New York.

20. Fry, Bernard M.; Hernon, Peter. *Government publications: key papers.* (Guides to official publications; v.8) Elmsford, NY: Pergamon Press; 1981. 814p.

A collection of papers, previously published in professional journals, on topics of bibliographic control, acquisitions, classification, and cataloging of government publications.

21. Evans, L.H.; Vambery, J.T. Documents and publications of contemporary international governmental organizations. *Law Library Journal.* 64: 338–362; 1971 Aug.

Lists international organizations, describes their structure and notes problems involved in their publications. Includes a good reference list for further consultation for those interested in a more comprehensive look at dealing with international publications.

22. Relyea, Harold C.; Riley, Tom. Freedom of information developments around the world: a symposium. *Government Publications Review.* 10(1): 1983 Jan.–Feb.

This symposium was published as a special section of *Government Publications Review*.

23. Reynolds, Hugh. Bibliographic guide to issues of national and international government information policies. *Government Publications Review*. 11: 1–39; 1984.

Bibliographic review providing an introduction to some of the major issues comprising information policy.

24. *State Publications Index*. Englewood, CO: Information Handling Services.

Since around 1976 this index has covered state publications, for which microfiche copies are available. Indexes reports by subject, by agency, and by author.

25. *Index to Current Urban Documents*. Westport, CT: Greenwood Press.

Provides an index to documents from cities having a population greater than 100,000 as well as to twenty-six counties. Has a subject approach and a geographical approach. Microfiche copies are available.

26. *CIS/Index to Publications of the United States Congress*. Washington: Congressional Information Service.

Published since 1970, this index provides for searching by subjects, personal names, document number, committee names, etc. Includes all House and Senate documents, with hearings indexed for each person who testifies. Microfiche copies are available; the index is also available as an online database (CIS).

Appendix A

Freedom of Information Act

U.S.C. §552: as amended

§522. Public information; agency rules, opinions, orders, records, and proceedings

(a) Each agency shall make available to the public information as follows:

(1) Each agency shall separately state and currently publish in the Federal Register for the guidance of the public—

(A) descriptions of its central and field organization and the established places at which, the employees (and in the case of a uniformed service, the members) from whom, and the methods whereby, the public may obtain information, make submittals or requests, or obtain decisions;

(B) statements of the general course and method by which its functions are channeled and determined, including the nature and requirements of all formal and informal procedures available;

(C) rules of procedure, descriptions of forms available or the places at which forms may be obtained, and instructions as to the scope and contents of all papers, reports, or examinations;

(D) substantive rules of general applicability adopted as authorized by law, and statements of general policy or interpretations of general applicability formulated and adopted by the agency; and

(E) each amendment, revision, or repeal of the foregoing.

Except to the extent that a person has actual and timely notice of the terms thereof, a person may not in any manner be required to resort to, or be adversely affected by, a matter required to be published in the Federal Register and not so published. For the purpose of this paragraph, matter reasonably available to the class of persons affected thereby is deemed published in the Federal Register when incorporated by reference therein with the approval of the Director of the Federal Register.

(2) Each agency, in accordance with published rules, shall make available for public inspection and copying—

(A) final opinions, including concurring and dissenting opinions, as well as orders, made in the adjudication of cases;

(B) those statements of policy and interpretations which have been adopted by the agency and are not published in the Federal Register; and

(C) administrative staff manuals and instructions to staff that affect a member of the public;

unless the materials are promptly published and copies offered for sale. To the extent required to prevent a clearly unwarranted invasion of personal privacy, an agency may delete identifying details when it makes available or publishes an opinion, statement of policy, interpretation, or staff manual or instruction. However, in each case the justification for the deletion shall be explained fully in writing. Each agency shall also maintain and make available for public inspection and copying current indexes providing identifying information for the public as to any matter issued, adopted, or promulgated after July 4, 1967, and required by this paragraph to be made available or published. Each agency shall promptly publish, quarterly or more frequently, and distribute (by sale or otherwise) copies of each index or supplements thereto unless it determines by order published in the Federal Register that the publication would be unnecessary and impracticable, in which case the agency shall nonetheless provide copies of such index on request at a cost not to exceed the direct cost of duplication. A final order, opinion, statement of policy, interpretation, or staff manual or instruction that affects a member of the public may be relied on, used, or cited as precedent by an agency against a party other than an agency only if—

(i) it has been indexed and either made available or published as provided by this paragraph; or

(ii) the party has actual and timely notice of the terms thereof.

(3) Except with respect to the records made available under paragraphs (1) and (2) of this subsection, each agency, upon any request for records which (A) reasonably describes such records and (B) is made in accordance with published rules stating the time, place, fees (if any), and procedures to be followed, shall make the records promptly available to any person.

(4) (A) In order to carry out the provisions of this section, each agency shall promulgate regulations, pursuant to notice and receipt of public comment, specifying a uniform schedule of fees applicable to all constituent units of such agency. Such fees shall be limited to reasonable standard charges for document search and duplication and provide for recovery of only the direct costs of such search and duplication. Documents shall be furnished without charge or at a reduced charge where the agency determines that waiver or reduction of the fee is in the public interest because furnishing the information can be considered as primarily benefiting the general public.

(B) On complaint, the district court of the United States in the district in which the complainant resides, or has his principal place of business, or in which the agency records are situated, or in the District of Columbia, has jurisdiction to enjoin the agency from withholding agency records and to order the production of any agency records improperly withheld from the complainant. In such a case the court shall determine the matter de novo, and may examine the contents of such agency records in camera to determine whether such records or any part thereof shall be withheld under any of the exemptions set forth in subsection (b) of this section, and the burden is on the agency to sustain its action.

(C) Notwithstanding any other provision of law, the defendant shall serve an answer or otherwise plead to any complaint made under this subsection within thirty days after service upon the defendant of the pleading in which such complaint is made, unless the court otherwise directs for good cause shown.

(D) Except as to cases the court considers of greater importance, proceedings before the district court, as authorized by this subsection, and appeals therefrom, take precedence on the docket over all cases and shall be assigned for hearing and trial or for argument at the earliest practicable date and expedited in every way.

(E) The court may assess against the United States reasonable attorney fees and other litigation costs reasonably incurred in any case under this section in which the complainant has substantially prevailed.

(F) Whenever the court orders the production of any agency

records improperly withheld from the complainant and assesses against the United States reasonable attorney fees and other litigation costs, and the court additionally issues a written finding that the circumstances surrounding the withholding raise questions whether agency personnel acted arbitrarily or capriciously with respect to the withholding, the Special Counsel shall promptly initiate a proceeding to determine whether disciplinary action is warranted against the officer or employee who was primarily responsible for the withholding. The Special Counsel, after investigation and consideration of the evidence submitted, shall submit his findings and recommendations to the administrative authority of the agency concerned and shall send copies of the findings and recommendations to the officer or employee or his representative. The administrative authority shall take the corrective action that the Special Counsel recommends.

(G) In the event of noncompliance with the order of the court, the district court may punish for contempt the responsible employee, and in the case of a uniformed service, the responsible member.

(5) Each agency having more than one member shall maintain and make available for public inspection a record of the final votes of each member in every agency proceeding.

(6) (A) Each agency, upon any request for records made under paragraph (1), (2), or (3) of this subsection, shall—

(i) determine within ten days (excepting Saturdays, Sundays, and legal public holidays) after the receipt of any such request whether to comply with such request and shall immediately notify the person making such request of such determination and the reasons therefor, and of the right of such person to appeal to the head of the agency any adverse determination; and

(ii) make a determination with respect to any appeal within twenty days (excepting Saturdays, Sundays, and legal public holidays) after the receipt of such appeal. If on appeal the denial of the request for records is in whole or in part upheld, the agency shall notify the person making such request of the provisions for judicial review of that determination under paragraph (4) of this subsection.

(B) In unusual circumstances as specified in this subparagraph, the time limits prescribed in either clause (i) or clause (ii) of subparagraph (A) may be extended by written notice of the person making such request setting forth the reasons for such extension and the date on which a determination is expected to be dispatched. No such notice shall specify a date that would result in an extension for more than ten working days. As used in this subparagraph, "unusual circumstances" means, but only to the extent reasonably necessary to the proper processing of the particular request—

(i) the need to search for and collect the requested records from field facilities or other establishments that are separate from the office processing the request;

(ii) the need to search for, collect, and appropriately examine a voluminous amount of separate and distinct records which are demanded in a single request; or

(iii) the need for consultation, which shall be conducted with all practicable speed, with another agency having a substantial interest in the determination of the request or among two or more components of the agency having substantial subject-matter interest therein.

(C) Any person making a request to any agency for records under paragraph (1), (2), or (3) of this subsection shall be deemed to have exhausted his administrative remedies with respect to such request if the agency fails to comply with the applicable time limit provisions of this paragraph. If the Government can show exceptional circumstances exist and that the agency is exercising due diligence in responding to the request, the court may retain jurisdiction and allow the agency additional time to complete its review of the records. Upon any determination by an agency to comply with a request for records, the records shall be made promptly available to such person making such request. Any notification of denial of any request for records under this subsection shall set forth the names and titles or positions of each person responsible for the denial of such request.

(b) This section does not apply to matters that are—

(1) (A) specifically authorized under criteria established by an Executive order to be kept secret in the interest of national defense or foreign policy and (B) are in fact properly classified pursuant to such Executive order;

(2) related solely to the internal personnel rules and practices of an agency;

(3) specifically exempted from disclosure by statute (other than section 552b of this title), provided that such statute (A) requires that the matters be withheld from the public in such a manner as to leave

no discretion on the issue, or (B) establishes particular criteria for withholding or refers to particular types of matters to be withheld;

(4) trade secrets and commercial or financial information obtained from a person and privileged or confidential;

(5) inter-agency or intra-agency memorandums or letters which would not be available by law to a party other than an agency in litigation with the agency;

(6) personnel and medical files and similar files the disclosure of which would constitute a clearly unwarranted invasion of personal privacy;

(7) investigatory records compiled for law enforcement purposes, but only to the extent that the production of such records would (A) interfere with enforcement proceedings, (B) deprive a person of a right to a fair trial or an impartial adjudication, (C) constitute an unwarranted invasion of personal privacy, (D) disclose the identity of a confidential source and, in the case of a record compiled by a criminal law enforcement authority in the course of a criminal investigation, or by an agency conducting a lawful national security intelligence investigation, confidential information furnished only by the confidential source, (E) disclose investigative techniques and procedures, or (F) endanger the life or physical safety of law enforcement personnel;

(8) contained in or related to examination, operating, or condition reports prepared by, on behalf of, or for the use of an agency responsible for the regulation or supervision of financial institutions; or

(9) geological and geophysical information and data, including maps, concerning wells.

Any reasonably segregable portion of a record shall be provided to any person requesting such record after deletion of the portions which are exempt under this subsection.

(c) This section does not authorize withholding of information or limit the availability of records to the public, except as specifically stated in this section. This section is not authority to withhold information from Congress.

(d) On or before March 1 of each calendar year, each agency shall submit a report covering the preceding calendar year to the Speaker of the House of Representatives and President of the Senate for referral to the appropriate committees of the Congress. The report shall include—

(1) the number of determinations made by such agency not to comply with requests for records made to such agency under subsection (a) and the reasons for each such determination;

(2) the number of appeals made by persons under subsection (a)
(6), the result of such appeals, and the reason for the action upon each
appeal that results in a denial of information;

(3) the names and titles or positions of each person responsible
for the denial of records requested under this section, and the number
of instances of participation for each;

(4) the results of each proceeding conducted pursuant to subsection (a)(4)(F), including a report of the disciplinary action taken
against the officer or employee who was primarily responsible for
improperly withholding records or an explanation of why disciplinary action was not taken;

(5) a copy of every rule made by such agency regarding this
section;

(6) a copy of the fee schedule and the total amount of fees collected by the agency for making records available under this section;
and

(7) such other information as indicates efforts to administer fully
this section.

The Attorney General shall submit an annual report on or before
March 1 of each calendar year which shall include for the prior
calendar year a listing of the number of cases arising under this
section, the exemption involved in each case, the disposition of such
case, and the cost, fees, and penalties assessed under subsections
(a)(4)(E), (F), and (G). Such report shall also include a description of
the efforts undertaken by the Department of Justice to encourage
agency compliance with this section.

(e) For purposes of this section, the term "agency" as defined in
section 551(1) of this title includes any executive department, military
department, Government corporation, Government controlled corporation, or other establishment in the executive branch of the Government (including the Executive Office of the President), or any independent regulatory agency.

Appendix B

Privacy Act of 1974

§552a. Records maintained on individuals
    (a) Definitions.
    For purposes of this section—
    (1) the term "agency" means agency as defined in section 552(e) of this title;
    (2) the term "individual" means a citizen of the United States or an alien lawfully admitted for permanent residence;
    (3) the term "maintain" includes maintain, collect, use or disseminate;
    (4) the term "record" means any item, collection, or grouping of information about an individual that is maintained by an agency, including, but not limited to, his education, financial transactions, medical history, and criminal or employment history and that contains his name, or the identifying number, symbol, or other identifying particular assigned to the individual, such as a finger or voice print or a photograph;
    (5) the term "system of records" means a group of any records under the control of any agency from which information is retrieved by the name of the individual or by some identifying number, symbol, or other identifying particular assigned to the individual;
    (6) the term "statistical record" means a record in a system of records maintained for statistical research or reporting purposes only and not used in whole or in part in making any determination about an identifiable individual, except as provided by section 8 of title 13; and

(7) the term "routine use" means, with respect to the disclosure of a record, the use of such record for a purpose which is compatible with the purpose for which it was collected.

(b) Conditions of disclosure.

No agency shall disclose any record which is contained in a system of records by any means of communication to any person, or to another agency, except pursuant to a written request by, or with the prior written consent of, the individual to whom the record pertains, unless disclosure of the record would be—

(1) to those officers and employees of the agency which maintains the record who have a need for the record in the performance of their duties;

(2) required under section 552 of this title;

(3) for a routine use as defined in subsection (a)(7) of this section and described under subsection (e)(4)(D) of this section;

(4) to the Bureau of the Census for purposes of planning or carrying out a census or survey or related activity pursuant to the provisions of title 13;

(5) to a recipient who has provided the agency with advance adequate written assurance that the record will be used solely as a statistical research or reporting record, and the record is to be transferred in a form that is not individually identifiable;

(6) to the National Archives of the United States as a record which has sufficient historical or other value to warrant its continued preservation by the United States Government, or for evaluation by the Administrator of General Services or his designee to determine whether the record has such value;

(7) to another agency or to an instrumentality of any governmental jurisdiction within or under the control of the United States for a civil or criminal law enforcement activity if the activity is authorized by law, and if the head of the agency or instrumentality has made a written request to the agency which maintains the record specifying the particular portion desired and the law enforcement activity for which the record is sought;

(8) to a person pursuant to a showing of compelling circumstances affecting the health or safety of an individual if upon such disclosure notification is transmitted to the last known address of such individual;

(9) to either House of Congress, or, to the extent of matter within its jurisdiction, any committee or subcommittee thereof, any joint committee of Congress or subcommittee of any such joint committee;

(10) to the Comptroller General, or any of his authorized rep-

resentatives, in the course of the performance of the duties of the General Accounting Office;

(11) pursuant to the order of a court of competent jurisdiction;

(12) to a consumer reporting agency in accordance with section 3711(f) of title 31.

(c) Accounting of Certain Disclosures

Each agency, with respect to each system of records under its control shall—

(1) except for disclosures made under subsections (b)(1) or (b)(2) of this section, keep an accurate accounting of—

(A) the date, nature, and purpose of each disclosure of a record to any person or to another agency made under subsection (b) of this section; and

(B) the name and address of the person or agency to whom the disclosure is made;

(2) retain the accounting made under paragraph (1) of this subsection for at least five years or the life of the record, whichever is longer, after the disclosure for which the accounting is made;

(3) except for disclosures made under subsection (b)(7) of this section, make the accounting made under paragraph (1) of this subsection available to the individual named in the record at his request; and

(4) inform any person or other agency about any correction or notation of dispute made by the agency in accordance with subsection (d) of this section of any record that has been disclosed to the person or agency if an accounting of the disclosure was made.

(d) Access to records

Each agency that maintains a system of records shall—

(1) upon request by any individual to gain access to his record or to any information pertaining to him which is contained in the system, permit him and upon his request, a person of his own choosing to accompany him, to review the record and have a copy made of all or any portion thereof in a form comprehensible to him, except that the agency may require the individual to furnish a written statement authorizing discussion of that individual's record in the accompanying person's presence;

(2) permit the individual to request amendment of a record pertaining to him and—

(A) not later than 10 days (excluding Saturdays, Sundays, and legal public holidays) after the date of receipt of such request, acknowledge in writing such receipt; and

(B) promptly, either—

(i) make any correction of any portion thereof which the individual believes is not accurate, relevant, timely, or complete; or

(ii) inform the individual of its refusal to amend the record in accordance with his request, the reason for the refusal, the procedures established by the agency for the individual to request a review of that refusal by the head of the agency or an officer designated by the head of the agency, and the name and business address of that official;

(3) permit the individual who disagrees with the refusal of the agency to amend his record to request a review of such refusal, and not later than 30 days (excluding Saturdays, Sundays, and legal public holidays) from the date on which the individual requests such review, complete such review and make a final determination unless, for good cause shown, the head of the agency extends such 30-day period; and if, after his review, the reviewing official also refuses to amend the record in accordance with the request, permit the individual to file with the agency a concise statement setting forth the reasons for his disagreement with the refusal of the agency, and notify the individual of the provisions for judicial review of the reviewing official's determination under subsection (g)(1)(A) of this section;

(4) in any disclosure, containing information about which the individual has filed a statement of disagreement, occurring after the filing of the statement under paragraph (3) of this subsection, clearly note any portion of the record which is disputed and provide copies of the statement and, if the agency deems it appropriate, copies of a concise statement of the reasons of the agency for not making the amendments requested, to persons or other agencies to whom the disputed record has been disclosed; and

(5) nothing in this section shall allow an individual access to any information compiled in reasonable anticipation of a civil action or proceeding.

(e) Agency requirements

Each agency that maintains a system of records shall—

(1) maintain in its records only such information about an individual as is relevant and necessary to accomplish a purpose of the agency required to be accomplished by statute or by executive order of the President;

(2) collect information to the greatest extent practicable directly from the subject individual when the information may result in

adverse determinations about an individual's rights, benefits, and privileges under Federal programs;

(3) inform each individual whom it asks to supply information, on the form which it uses to collect the information or on a separate form that can be retained by the individual—

(A) the authority (whether granted by statute, or by executive order of the President) which authorizes the solicitation of the information and whether disclosure of such information is mandatory or voluntary;

(B) the principal purpose or purposes for which the information is intended to be used;

(C) the routine uses which may be made of the information, as published pursuant to paragraph (4)(D) of this subsection; and

(D) the effects on him, if any, of not providing all or any part of the requested information;

(4) subject to the provisions of paragraph (11) of this subsection, publish in the Federal Register upon establishment or revision a notice of the existence and character of the system of records, which notice shall include—

(A) the name and location of the system;

(B) the categories of individuals on whom records are maintained in the system;

(C) the categories of records maintained in the system;

(D) each routine use of the records contained in the system, including the categories of users and the purpose of such use;

(E) the policies and practices of the agency regarding storage, retrievability, access controls, retention, and disposal of the records;

(F) the title and business address of the agency official who is responsible for the system of records;

(G) the agency procedures whereby an individual can be notified at his request if the system of records contains a record pertaining to him;

(H) the agency procedures whereby an individual can be notified at his request how he can gain access to any record pertaining to him contained in the system of records, and how he can contest its content; and

(I) the categories of sources of records in the system;

(5) maintain all records which are used by the agency in making any determination about any individual with such accuracy, relevance, timeliness, and completeness as is reasonably necessary to assure fairness to the individual in the determination;

(6) prior to disseminating any record about an individual to any

person other than an agency, unless the dissemination is made pursuant to subsection (b)(2) of this section, make reasonable efforts to assure that such records are accurate, complete, timely, and relevant for agency purposes;

(7) maintain no record describing how any individual exercises rights guaranteed by the First Amendment unless expressly authorized by statute or by the individual about whom the record is maintained or unless pertinent to and within the scope of an authorized law enforcement activity;

(8) make reasonable efforts to serve notice on an individual when any record on such individual is made available to any person under compulsory legal process when such process becomes a matter of public record;

(9) establish rules of conduct for persons involved in the design, development, operation, or maintenance of any system of records, or in maintaining any record, and instruct each such person with respect to such rules and the requirements of this section, including any other rules and procedures adopted pursuant to this section and the penalties for noncompliance;

(10) establish appropriate administrative, technical and physical safeguards to insure the security and confidentiality of records and to protect against any anticipated threats or hazards to their security or integrity which could result in substantial harm, embarrassment, inconvenience, or unfairness to any individual on whom information is maintained; and

(11) at least 30 days prior to publication of information under paragraph (4)(D) of this subsection, publish in the Federal Register notice of any new use or intended use of the information in the system, and provide an opportunity for interested persons to submit written data, views, or arguments to the agency.

(f) Agency rules

In order to carry out the provisions of this section, each agency that maintains a system of records shall promulgate rules, in accordance with the requirements (including general notice) of section 553 of this title, which shall—

(1) establish procedures whereby an individual can be notified in response to his request if any system of records named by the individual contains a record pertaining to him;

(2) define reasonable times, places, and requirements for identifying an individual who requests his record or information pertaining to him before the agency shall make the record or information available to the individual;

(3) establish procedures for the disclosure to an individual upon his request of his record or information pertaining to him, including special procedure, if deemed necessary, for the disclosure to an individual of medical records, including psychological records pertaining to him;

(4) establish procedures for reviewing a request from an individual concerning the amendment of any record or information pertaining to the individual, for making a determination on the request, for an appeal within the agency of an initial adverse agency determination, and for whatever additional means may be necessary for each individual to be able to exercise fully his rights under this section; and

(5) establish fees to be charged, if any, to any individual for making copies of his record, excluding the cost of any search for and review of the record.

The Office of the Federal Register shall annually compile and publish the rules promulgated under this subsection and agency notices published under subsection (e)(4) of this section in a form available to the public at low cost.

(g)(1) Civil remedies

Whenever any agency

(A) makes a determination under subsection (d)(3) of this section not to amend an individual's record in accordance with his request, or fails to make such review in conformity with that subsection;

(B) refuses to comply with an individual request under subsection (d)(1) of this section;

(C) fails to maintain any record concerning any individual with such accuracy, relevance, timeliness, and completeness as is necessary to assure fairness in any determination relating to the qualifications, character, rights, or opportunities of, or benefits to the individual that may be made on the basis of such record, and consequently a determination is made which is adverse to the individual; or

(D) fails to comply with any other provision of this section, or any rule promulgated thereunder, in such a way as to have an adverse effect on an individual, the individual may bring a civil action against the agency, and the district courts of the United States shall have jurisdiction in the matters under the provisions of this subsection.

(2)(A) In any suit brought under the provisions of subsection (g)(1)(A) of this section, the court may order the agency to amend the individual's record in accordance with his request or in such other way as the court may direct. In such a case the court shall determine the matter de novo.

(B) The court may assess against the United States reasonable attorney fees and other litigation costs reasonably incurred in any case under this paragraph in which the complainant has substantially prevailed.

(3)(A) In any suit brought under the provisions of subsection (g)(1)(B) of this section, the court may enjoin the agency from withholding the records and order the production to the complainant of any agency records improperly withheld from him. In such a case the court shall determine the matter de novo, and may examine the contents of any agency records in camera to determine whether the records or portion thereof may be withheld under any of the exemptions set forth in subsection (k) of this section, and the burden is on the agency to sustain its action.

(B) The court may assess against the United States reasonable attorney fees and other litigation costs reasonably incurred in any case under this paragraph in which the complainant has substantially prevailed.

(4) In any suit brought under the provisions of subsection (g)(1)(C) or (D) of this section in which the court determines that the agency acted in a manner which was intentional or willful, the United States shall be liable to the individual in an amount equal to the sum of—

(A) actual damages sustained by the individual as a result of the refusal or failure, but in no case shall a person entitled to recovery receive less than the sum of $1,000; and

(B) the costs of the action together with reasonable attorney fees as determined by the court.

(5) An action to enforce any liability created under this section may be brought in the district court of the United States in the district in which the complainant resides, or has his principal place of business, or in which the agency records are situated, or in the District of Columbia, without regard to the amount in controversy, within two years from the date on which the cause of action arises, except that where an agency has materially and willfully misrepresented any information required under this section to be disclosed to an individual and the information so misrepresented is material to establishment of the liability of the agency to the individual under this section, the action may be brought at any time within two years after discovery by the individual of the misrepresentation. Nothing in this section shall be construed to authorize any civil action by reason of any injury sustained as the result of a disclosure of a record prior to September 27, 1975.

(h) Rights of legal guardians

For the purposes of this section, the parent of any minor, or the legal guardian of any individual who has been declared to be incompetent due to physical or mental incapacity or age by a court of competent jurisdiction, may act on behalf of the individual.

(i)(1) Criminal penalties

Any officer or employee of an agency, who by virtue of his employment or official position, has possession of, or access to, agency records which contain individually identifiable information the disclosure of which is prohibited by this section or by rules or regulations established thereunder, and who knowing that disclosure of the specific material is so prohibited, willfully discloses the material in any manner to any person or agency not entitled to receive it, shall be guilty of a misdemeanor and fined not more than $5,000.

(2) Any officer or employee of any agency who willfully maintains a system of records without meeting the notice requirements of subsection (e)(4) of this section shall be guilty of a misdemeanor and fined not more than $5,000.

(3) Any person who knowingly and willfully requests or obtains any record concerning an individual from an agency under false pretenses shall be guilty of a misdemeanor and fined not more than $5,000.

(j) General exemptions

The head of any agency may promulgate rules, in accordance with the requirements (including general notice) of sections 553(b)(1), (2), and (3), (c), and (e) of this title, to exempt any system of records within the agency from any part of this sections except subsections (b), (c)(1) and (2), (e)(4)(A) through (F), (e)(6), (7), (9), (10), and (11), and (i) if the system of records is—

(1) maintained by the Central Intelligence Agency; or

(2) maintained by an agency or component thereof which performs as its principal function any activity pertaining to the enforcement of criminal laws, including police efforts to prevent, control, or reduce crime or to apprehend criminals, and the activities of prosecutors, courts, correctional, probation, pardon, or parole authorities, and which consists of (A) information compiled for the purpose of identifying individual criminal offenders and alleged offenders and consisting only of identifying data and notations of arrests, the nature and disposition of criminal charges, sentencing, confinement, release, and parole and probation status; (B) information compiled for the purpose of a criminal investigation, including reports of informants and investigators, and associated with an identifiable individual; or (C) reports identifiable to an individual compiled at any stage of the

process of enforcement of the criminal laws from arrest or indictment through release from supervision.

At the time rules are adopted under this subsection, the agency shall include in the statement required under section 553(c) of this title, the reasons why the system of records is to be exempted from a provision of this section.

(k) Specific exemptions

The head of any agency may promulgate rules, in accordance with the requirements (including general notice) of sections 553(b)(1), (2), and (3), (c), and (e) of this title, to exempt any system of records within the agency from subsections (c)(3), (d), (e)(1), (e)(4)(G), (H), and (I) and (f) of this section if the system of records is—

(1) subject to the provisions of section 552(b)(1) of this title;

(2) investigatory material compiled for law enforcement purposes, other than material within the scope of subsection (j)(2) of this section; PROVIDED, HOWEVER, That if any individual is denied any right, privilege, or benefit that he would otherwise be entitled by Federal law, or for which he would otherwise be eligible, as a result of the maintenance of such material, such material shall be provided to such individual, except to the extent that the disclosure of such material would reveal the identity of a source who furnished information to the Government under an express promise that the identity of the source would be held in confidence, or, prior to the effective date of this section, under an implied promise that the identity of the source would be held in confidence;

(3) maintained in connection with providing protective services to the President of the United States or other individuals pursuant to section 3056 of title 18;

(4) required by statute to be maintained and used solely as statistical records;

(5) investigatory material compiled solely for the purpose of determining suitability, eligibility, or qualifications for Federal civilian employment, military service, Federal contracts, or access to classified information, but only to the extent that the disclosure of such material would reveal the identity of a source who furnished information to the Government under an express promise that the identity of the source would be held in confidence, or, prior to the effective date of this section, under an implied promise that the identity of the source would be held in confidence;

(6) testing or examination material used solely to determine individual qualifications for appointment or promotion in the Fed-

eral service the disclosure of which would compromise the objectivity or fairness of the testing or examination process; or

(7) evaluation material used to determine potential for promotion in the armed services, but only to the extent that the disclosure of such material would reveal the identity of a source who furnished information to the Government under an express promise that the identity of the source would be held in confidence, or, prior to the effective date of this section, under an implied promise that the identity of the source would be held in confidence.

At the time rules are adopted under this subsection, the agency shall include in the statement required under section 553(c) of this title, the reasons why the system of records is to be exempted from a provision of this section.

(l)(1)Archival records

Each agency record which is accepted by the Administrator of General Services for storage, processing, and servicing in accordance with section 3103 of title 44 shall, for the purposes of this section, be considered to be maintained by the agency which deposited the record and shall be subject to the provisions of this section. The Administrator of General Services shall not disclose the record except to the agency which maintains the record, or under rules established by that agency which are not inconsistent with the provisions of this section.

(2) Each agency record pertaining to an identifiable individual which was transferred to the National Archives of the United States as a record which has sufficient historical or other value to warrant its continued preservation by the United States Government, prior to the effective date of this section, shall, for the purposes of this section, be considered to be maintained by the National Archives and shall not be subject to the provisions of this section, except that a statement generally describing such records (modeled after the requirements relating to records subject to subsections (e)(4)(A) through (G) of this section) shall be published in the Federal Register.

(3) Each agency record pertaining to an identifiable individual which is transferred to the National Archives of the United States as a record which has sufficient historical or other value to warrant its continued preservation by the United States Government, on or after the effective date of this section, maintained by the National Archives and shall be exempt from the requirements of this section except subsections (e)(4)(A) through (G) and (e)(9) of this section.

(m) Government contractors

(1) When an agency provides by a contract for the operation by or on behalf of the agency of a system of records to accomplish an agency function, the agency shall, consistent with its authority, cause the requirements of this section to be applied to such system. For purposes of subsection (i) of this section any such contractor and any employee of such contractor, if such contract is agreed to on or after the effective date of this section, shall be considered to be an employee of an agency.

(2) A consumer reporting agency to which a record is disclosed under section 3711(f) of title 31 shall not be considered a contractor for the purposes of this section.

(n) Mailing lists

An individual's name and address may not be sold or rented by an agency unless such action is specifically authorized by law. This provision shall not be construed to require the withholding of names and addresses otherwise permitted to be made public.

(o) Report on new systems

Each agency shall provide adequate advance notice to Congress and the Office of Management and Budget of any proposal to establish or alter any system of records in order to permit an evaluation of the probable or potential effect of such proposal on the privacy and other personal or property rights of individuals or the disclosure of information relating to such individuals, and its effect on the preservation of the constitutional principles of federalism and separation of powers.

(p) Annual report

The President shall annually submit to the Speaker of the House of Representatives and the President pro tempore of the Senate a report—

(1) describing the actions of the Director of the Office of Management and Budget pursuant to section 6 of the Privacy Act of 1974 during the preceding year;

(2) describing the exercise of individual rights of access and amendment under this section during such year;

(3) identifying changes in or additions to systems of records;

(4) containing such other information concerning administration of this section as may be necessary or useful to the Congress in reviewing the effectiveness of this section in carrying out the purposes of the Privacy Act of 1974.

(q) Effect of other laws

No agency shall rely on any exemption contained in section 552 of this title to withhold from an individual any record which is otherwise accessible to such individual under the provisions of this section.

The following sections were originally part of the Privacy Act but were not codified:

Sec. 6 The Office of Management and Budget shall—

(1) develop guidelines and regulations for the use of agencies in implementing the provisions of section 552a of title 5, United States Code, as added by section 3 of this Act; and

(2) provide continuing assistance to and oversight of the implementation of the provisions of such section by agencies.

Sec. 7 (a)(1) It shall be unlawful for any Federal, State or local government agency to deny to any individual any right, benefit, or privilege provided by law because of such individual's refusal to disclose his social security account number.

(2) the provisions of paragraph (1) of this subsection shall not apply with respect to—

(A) any disclosure which is required by Federal statute, or

(B) any disclosure of a social security number to any Federal, State, or local agency maintaining a system of records in existence and operating before January 1, 1975, if such disclosure was required under statute or regulation adopted prior to such date to verify the identity of an individual.

(b) Any Federal, State or local government agency which requests an individual to disclose his social security account number shall inform that individual whether that disclosure is mandatory or voluntary, by what statutory or other authority such number is solicited, and what uses will be made of it.

Government in the Sunshine Act

5 U.S.C. §552b

§552b. Open meetings

(a) For purposes of this section—

(1) the term "agency" means any agency, as defined in section 552(e) of this title, headed by a collegial body composed of two or more individual members, a majority of whom are appointed to such position by the President with the advice and consent of the Senate, and any subdivision thereof authorized to act on behalf of the agency;

(2) the term "meeting" means the deliberations of at least the number of individual agency members required to take action on behalf of the agency where such deliberations determine or result in the joint conduct or disposition of official agency business, but does not include deliberations required or permitted by subsection (d) or (e); and

(3) the term "member" means an individual who belongs to a collegial body heading an agency.

(b) Members shall not jointly conduct or dispose of agency business other than in accordance with this section. Except as provided in subsection (c), every portion of every meeting of an agency shall be open to public observation.

(c) Except in a case where the agency finds that the public interest requires otherwise, the second sentence of subsection (b) shall not apply to any portion of an agency meeting, and the requirements of subsections (d) and (e) shall not apply to any information pertaining to such meeting otherwise required by this section to be disclosed to the public, where the agency properly determines that such portion or portions of its meeting or the disclosure of such information is likely to—

(1) disclose matters that are (A) specifically authorized under criteria established by an Executive order to be kept secret in the interests of national defense or foreign policy and (B) in fact properly classified pursuant to such Executive order;

(2) relate solely to the internal personnel rules and practices of an agency;

(3) disclose matters specifically exempted from disclosure by statute (other than section 552 of this title), provided that such statute (A) requires that the matters be withheld from the public in such a manner as to leave no discretion on the issue, or (B) establishes particular criteria for withholding or refers to particular types of matters to be withheld;

(4) disclose trade secrets and commercial or financial information obtained from a person and privileged or confidential;

(5) involve accusing any person of a crime, or formally censuring any person;

(6) disclose information of a personal nature where disclosure would constitute a clearly unwarranted invasion of personal privacy;

(7) disclose investigatory records compiled for law enforcement purposes, or information which if written would be contained in such records, but only to the extent that the production of such records or information would (A) interfere with enforcement proceedings, (B) deprive a person of a right to a fair trial or an impartial adjudication, (C) constitute an unwarranted invasion of personal privacy, (D) disclose the identity of a confidential source and, in the case of a record compiled by a criminal law enforcement authority in the course of a criminal investigation, or by an agency conducting a lawful national security intelligence investigation, confidential information furnished only by the confidential source, (E) disclose investigative techniques and procedures, or (F) endanger the life or physical safety of law enforcement personnel;

(8) disclose information contained in or related to examination, operating or condition reports prepared by, on behalf of, or for the use of an agency responsible for the regulation or supervision of financial institutions;

(9) disclose information the premature disclosure of which would—

(A) in the case of an agency which regulates currencies, securities, commodities, or financial institutions, be likely to (i) lead to significant financial speculation in currencies, securities, or commodities, or (ii) significantly endanger the stability of any financial institution; or

(B) in the case of any agency, be likely to significantly frustrate implementation of a proposed agency action.

except that subparagraph (B) shall not apply in any instance where the agency has already disclosed to the public the content or nature of its proposed action, or where the agency is required by law to make such disclosure on its own initiative prior to taking final agency action on such proposal; or

(10) specifically concern the agency's issuance of a subpoena, or the agency's participation in a civil action proceeding, an action in a foreign court or international tribunal, or an arbitration, or the initiation, conduct, or disposition by the agency of a particular case of formal agency adjudication pursuant to the procedures in section 554 of this title or otherwise involving a determination on the record after opportunity for a hearing.

(d)(1) Action under subsection (c) shall be taken only when a majority of the entire membership of the agency (as defined in subsection (a)(1))votes to take such action. A separate vote of the agency members shall be taken with respect to each agency meeting a portion or portions of which are proposed to be closed to the public pursuant to subsection (c), or with respect to any information which is proposed to be withheld under subsection (c). A single vote may be taken with respect to a series of meetings, a portion or portions of which are proposed to be closed to the public, or with respect to any information concerning such series of meetings, so long as each meeting in such series involves the same particular matters and is scheduled to be held no more than thirty days after the initial meeting in such series. The vote of each agency member participating in such vote shall be recorded and no proxies shall be allowed.

(2) Whenever any person whose interests may be directly affected by a portion of a meeting requests that the agency close such portion to the public for any of the reasons referred to in paragraph (5), (6), or (7) of subsection (c), the agency, upon request of any one of its members, shall vote by recorded vote whether to close such meeting.

(3) Within one day of any vote taken pursuant to paragraph (1) or (2), the agency shall make publicly available a written copy of such vote reflecting the vote of each member on the question. If a portion of a meeting is to be closed to the public, the agency shall, within one

day of the vote taken pursuant to paragraph (1) or (2) of this subsection, make publicly available a full written explanation of its action closing the portion together with a list of all persons expected to attend the meeting and their affiliation.

(4) Any agency, a majority of whose meetings may properly be closed to the public pursuant to paragraph (4), (8), (9)(A), or (10) of subsection (c), or any combination thereof may provide by regulation for the closing of such meetings or portions thereof in the event that a majority of the members of the agency votes by recorded vote at the beginning of such meeting, or portion thereof, to close the exempt portion or portions of the meeting, and a copy of such vote, reflecting the vote of each member on the question, is made available to the public. The provisions of paragraphs (1), (2), and (3) of this subsection and subsection (e) shall not apply to any portion of a meeting to which such regulations apply; PROVIDED, That the agency shall, except to the extent that such information is exempt from disclosure under the provisions of subsection (c), provide the public with public announcement of the time, place, and subject matter of the meeting and of each portion thereof at the earliest practicable time.

(e)(1) In the case of each meeting, the agency shall make public announcement, at least one week before the meeting, of the time, place, and subject matter of the meeting, whether it is to be open or closed to the public, and the name and phone number of the official designated by the agency to respond to requests for information about the meeting. Such announcement shall be made unless a majority of the members of the agency determines by a recorded vote that agency business requires that such meeting be called at an earlier date, in which case the agency shall make public announcement of the time, place, and subject matter of such meeting, and whether open or closed to the public, at the earliest practicable time.

(2) The time or place of a meeting may be changed following the public announcement required by paragraph (1) only if the agency publicly announces such change at the earliest practicable time. The subject matter of a meeting, or the determination of the agency to open or close a meeting, or portion of a meeting, to the public, may be changed following the public announcement required by this subsection only if (A) a majority of the entire membership of the agency determines by a recorded vote that agency business so requires and that no earlier announcement of the change was possible, and (B) the agency publicly announces such change and the vote of each member upon such change at the earliest practicable time.

(3) Immediately following each public announcement required

by this subsection, notice of the time, place, and subject matter of a meeting, whether the meeting is open or closed, any change in one of the preceding, and the name and phone number of the official designated by the agency to respond to requests for information about the meeting, shall also be submitted for publication in the Federal Register.

(f)(1) For every meeting closed pursuant to paragraphs (1) through (10) of subsection (c), the General Counsel or chief legal officer of the agency shall publicly certify that, in his or her opinion, the meeting may be closed to the public and shall state each relevant exemptive provision. A copy of such certification, together with a statement from the presiding officer of the meeting setting forth the time and place of the meeting, and the persons present, shall be retained by the agency. The agency shall maintain a complete transcript or electronic recording adequate to record fully the proceedings of each meeting, or portion of a meeting, closed to the public, except that in the case of a meeting, or portion of a meeting closed to the public pursuant to paragraph (8), (9)(A), or (10) of subsection (c), the agency shall maintain either such a transcript or recording, or a set of minutes. Such minutes shall fully and clearly describe all matters discussed and shall provide a full and accurate summary of any actions taken, and the reasons therefor, including a description of each of the views expressed on any item and the record of any roll call vote (reflecting the vote of each member on the question). All documents considered in connection with any action shall be identified in such minutes.

(2) The agency shall make promptly available to the public, in a place easily accessible to the public, the transcript, electronic recording, or minutes (as required by paragraph (1)) of the discussion of any item on the agenda, or of any item of the testimony of any witness received at the meeting, except for such item or items of such discussion or testimony as the agency determines to contain information which may be withheld under subsection (c). Copies of such transcript, or minutes, or a transcription of such recording disclosing the identity of each speaker, shall be furnished to any person at the actual cost of duplication or transcription. The agency shall maintain a complete verbatim copy of the transcript, a complete copy of the minutes, or a complete electronic recording of each meeting, or portion of a meeting, closed to the public, for a period of at least two years after such meeting, or until one year after the conclusion of any agency proceeding with respect to which the meeting or portion was held, whichever occurs later.

(g) Each agency subject to the requirements of this section shall, within 180 days after the date of enactment of this section, following consultation with the Office of the Chairman of the Administrative Conference of the United States and published notice in the Federal Register of at least thirty days and opportunity for written comment by any person, promulgate regulations to implement the requirements of subsections (b) through (f) of this section. Any person may bring a proceeding in the United States District Court for the District of Columbia to require an agency to promulgate such regulations if such agency has not promulgated such regulations within the time period specified herein. Subject to any limitations of time provided by law, any person may bring a proceeding in the United States Court of Appeals for the District of Columbia to set aside agency regulations issued pursuant to this subsection that are not in accord with the requirements of subsections (b) through (f) of this section and to require the promulgation of regulations that are in accord with such subsections.

(h)(1) The district courts of the United States shall have jurisdiction to enforce the requirements of subsections (b) through (f) of this section by declaratory judgment, injunctive relief, or other relief as may be appropriate. Such actions may be brought by any person against an agency prior to, or within sixty days after, the meeting out of which the violation of this section arises, except that if public announcement of such meeting is not initially provided by the agency in accordance with the requirements of this section, such action may be instituted pursuant to this section at any time prior to sixty days after any public announcement of such meeting. Such actions may be brought in the district court of the United States for the district in which the agency meeting is held or in which the agency in question has its headquarters, or in the District Court for the District of Columbia. In such actions a defendant shall serve his answer within thirty days after the service of the complaint. The burden is on the defendant to sustain his action. In deciding such cases the court may examine in camera any portion of the transcript, electronic recording, or minutes of a meeting closed to the public, and may take such additional evidence as it deems necessary. The court, having due regard for orderly administration and the public interest, as well as the interests of the parties, may grant such equitable relief as it deems appropriate, including granting an injunction against future violations of this section or ordering the agency to make available to the public such portion of the transcript, recording or minutes of a meeting as is not authorized to be withheld under subsection (c) of this section.

(2) Any Federal court otherwise authorized by law to review agency action may, at the application of any person properly participating in the proceeding pursuant to other applicable law, inquire into violations by the agency of the requirements of this section and afford such relief as it deems appropriate. Nothing in this section authorizes any Federal court having jurisdiction solely on the basis of paragraph (1) to set aside, enjoin, or invalidate any agency action (other than an action to close a meeting or to withhold information under this section) taken or discussed at any agency meeting out of which the violation of this section arose.

(i) The court may assess against any party reasonable attorney fees and other litigation costs reasonably incurred by any other party who substantially prevails in any action brought in accordance with the provisions of subsection (g) or (h) of this section, except that costs may be assessed against the plaintiff only where the court finds that the suit was initiated by the plaintiff primarily for frivolous or dilatory purposes. In the case of assessment of costs against an agency, the costs may be assessed by the court against the United States.

(j) Each agency subject to the requirements of this section shall annually report to Congress regarding its compliance with such requirements, including a tabulation of the total number of agency meetings open to the public, the total number of meetings closed to the public, the reasons for closing such meetings, and a description of any litigation brought against the agency under this section, including any costs assessed against the agency in such litigation (whether or not paid by the agency).

(k) Nothing herein expands or limits the present rights of any person under section 552 of this title, except that the exemptions set forth in subsection (c) of this section shall govern in the case of any request made pursuant to section 552 to copy or inspect the transcripts, recordings, or minutes described in subsection (f) of this section. The requirements of chapter 33 of title 44, United States Code, shall not apply to the transcripts, recordings, and minutes described in subsection (f) of this section.

(l) This section does not constitute authority to withhold any information from Congress, and does not authorize the closing of any agency meeting or portion thereof required by any other provision of law to be open.

(m) Nothing in this section authorizes any agency to withhold from any individual any record, including transcripts, recordings, or minutes required by this section, which is otherwise accessible to such individual under section 552a of this title.

Extracts of the Espionage and Sabotage Acts and Other Federal Criminal Statutes

U.S.C. 18 - 793. Gathering, transmitting, or losing defense information

(a) Whoever, for the purpose of obtaining information respecting the national defense with intent or reason to believe that the information is to be used to the injury of the United States, or to the advantage of any foreign nation, goes upon, enters, flies over, or otherwise obtains information concerning any vessel, aircraft, work of defense, navy yard, naval station, submarine base, fueling station, fort, battery, torpedo station, dockyard, canal, railroad, arsenal, camp, factory, mine, telegraph, telephone, wireless, or signal station, building, office, research laboratory or station or other place connected with the national defense owned or constructed, or in progress of construction by the United States or under the control of the United States, or of any of its officers, departments, or agencies, or within the exclusive jurisdiction of the United States, or any place in which any vessel, aircraft, arms, munitions, or other materials or instruments for use in time of war are being made, prepared, repaired, stored, or are the subject of research or development, under any contract or agreement with the United States or any department or agency thereof or with any person on behalf of the United States, or otherwise on behalf of the United States, or any prohibited place as designated by the President by proclamation in time of war or in case of national emergency in which anything for the use of the Army, Navy, or Air Force is being prepared or constructed or stored, information as to which prohibited place the President has determined would be prejudicial to the national defense; or

(b) Whoever, for the purpose aforesaid, and with like intent or reason to believe, copies, takes, makes, or obtains, or attempts to copy, take, make, or obtain, any sketch, photograph, photographic negative, blueprint, plan, map, model, instrument, appliance, document, writing, or note of anything connected with the national defense; or

(c) Whoever, for the purpose aforesaid, receives or obtains or agrees or attempts to receive or obtain from any person, or from any source whatever, any document, writing, code book, signal book, sketch, photograph, photographic negative, blueprint, plan, map, model, instrument, appliance, or note of anything connected with the national defense, knowing or having reason to believe, at the time he receives or obtains, or agrees or attempts to receive or obtain it, that it has been or will be obtained, taken, made, or disposed of by any person contrary to the provisions of this chapter; or

(d) Whoever, lawfully having possession of, access to, control over, or being entrusted with any document, writing, code book, signal book, sketch, photograph, photographic negative, blueprint, plan, map, model, instrument, appliance, or note relating to the national defense, or information relating to the national defense which information the possessor has reason to believe could be used to the injury of the United States or the advantage of any foreign nation, willfully communicates, delivers, transmits or causes to be communicated, delivered, or transmitted or attempts to communicate, deliver, transmit or cause to be communicated, delivered or transmitted, the same to any person not entitled to receive it, or willfully retains the same and fails to deliver it on demand to the officer or employee of the United States entitled to receive it; or

(e) Whoever, having unauthorized possession of, access to or control over any document, writing, code book, signal book, sketch, photograph, photographic negative, blueprint, plan, map, model, instrument, appliance, or note relating to the national defense or information relating to the national defense which information the possessor has reason to believe could be used to the injury of the United States or to the advantage of any foreign nation, willfully communicates, delivers, transmits or causes to be communicated, delivered, or transmitted, or attempts to communicate, deliver, transmit or cause to be communicated, delivered, or transmitted the same to any person not entitled to receive it, or willfully retains the same and fails to deliver it to the officer or employee of the United States entitled to receive it; or

(f) Whoever, being entrusted with or having lawful possession or control of any document, writing, code book, signal book, sketch, photograph, photographic negative, blueprint, plan, map, model, instrument, appliance, note, or information, relating to the national defense, (1) through gross negligence permits the same to be removed from its proper place of custody or delivered to anyone in violation of his trust, or to be lost, stolen, abstracted, or destroyed, or (2) having knowledge that the same has been illegally removed from its proper place of custody or delivered to anyone in violation of his trust, or lost, or stolen, abstracted, or destroyed, and fails to make prompt report of such lose, theft, abstraction, or destruction to his superior officer—

Shall be fined not more than $10,000 or imprisoned not more than ten years, or both.

(g) If two or more persons conspire to violate any of the foregoing provisions of this section, and one or more of such persons do any act to effect the object of the conspiracy, each of the parties to such conspiracy shall be subject to the punishment provided for the offense which is the object of such conspiracy.

U.S.C. 18 - 794. Gathering or delivering defense information to aid foreign governments

(a) Whoever, with intent or reason to believe that it is to be used to the injury of the United States or to the advantage of a foreign nation, communicates, delivers, or transmits, or attempts to communicate, deliver, or transmit, to any foreign government, or to any faction or party or military or naval force within a foreign country, whether recognized or unrecognized by the United States, or to any representative, officer, agent, employee, subject, or citizen thereof, either directly or indirectly, any document, writing, code book, signal book, sketch, photograph, photographic negative, blueprint, plan, map, model, note, instrument, appliance, or information relating to the national defense, shall be punished by death or by imprisonment for any term of years or for life.

(b) Whoever, in time of war, with intent that the same shall be communicated to the enemy, collects, records, publishes, or communicates, or attempts to elicit any information with respect to the movement, numbers, description, condition, or disposition of any of the Armed Forces, ships, aircraft or war material of the United States, or with respect to the plans or conduct, or supposed plans or conduct of any naval or military operations, or with respect to any works or measures undertaken for or connected with, or intended for the fortification of defense of any place, or any other information relating to the public defense, which might be useful to the enemy, shall be punished by death or by imprisonment for any term of years or for life.

(c) If two or more persons conspire to violate this section, and one or more of such persons do any act to effect the object of the conspiracy, each of the parties to such conspiracy shall be subject to the punishment provided for the offense which is the object of such conspiracy.

U.S.C. 18 - 795. Photographing and sketching defense installations

(a) Whenever, in the interests of national defense, the President defines certain vital military or naval installations or equipments as requiring protection against the general dissemination of information relative thereto, it shall be unlawful to make any photograph, sketch, picture, drawing, map, or equipment without first obtaining permission of the commanding officer of the military or naval post, camp, or station, or naval vessels, military and naval aircraft, and any separate military or naval command concerned, or higher authority, and promptly submitting the product obtained to such commanding officer or higher authority for censorship or such other action as he may deem necessary.

(b) Whoever violates this section shall be fined not more than $1,000 or imprisoned not more than one year, or both.

U.S.C. 18 - 796. Use of aircraft for photographic defense installations

Whoever uses or permits the use of an aircraft or any contrivance used, or designed for navigation or flight in the air, for the purpose of making a photograph, sketch, picture, drawing, map, or graphical representation of vital military or naval installations or equipment, in violation of section 795 of this title, shall be fined not more than $1,000 or imprisoned not more than one year, or both.

U.S.C. 18 - 797. Publication and sale of photographs of defense installations

On and after 30 days from the date upon which the President defines any vital military or naval installation or equipment as being within the category contemplated under section 795 of this title, whoever reproduces, publishes, sells, or gives away any photograph, sketch, picture, drawing, map, or graphical representation of the vital military or naval installations or equipment so defined, without first obtaining permission of the commanding officer of the military or naval post, camp, or station concerned, or higher authority, unless such photograph, sketch, picture, drawing, map, or graphical representation has clearly indicated thereon that it has been censored by the proper military or naval authority, shall be fined not more than $1,000 or imprisoned not more than one year, or both.

U.S.C. 18 - 798. Disclosure of classified information

(a) Whoever knowingly and willfully communicates, furnishes, transmits, or otherwise makes available to an unauthorized person, or publishes, or uses in any manner prejudicial to the safety or interest of the United States or for the benefit of any foreign government to the detriment of the United States any classified information—

(1) concerning the nature, preparation, or use of any code, cipher, or cryptographic system of the United States or any foreign government; or

(2) concerning the design, construction, use, maintenance, or repair of any device, apparatus, or appliance used or prepared or planned for use by the United States or any foreign government for cryptographic or communication intelligence purposes; or

(3) concerning the communication intelligence activities of the United States or any foreign government; or

(4) obtained by the processes of communication intelligence from the communications of any foreign government, knowing the same to have been obtained by such processes—

Shall be fined not more than $10,000 or imprisoned not more than ten years, or both.

(b) As used in subsection (a) of this section—The term "classified information" means information which, at the time of a violation of this section, is, for reasons of national security, specifically designated by a United States Government Agency for limited or restricted dissemination or distribution;

The terms "code," "cipher," and "cryptographic system" include in their meanings, in addition to their usual meanings, any method of secret writing and any mechanical or electrical device or method used for the purpose of disguising or concealing the contents, significance, or meanings of communications;

The term "foreign government" includes in its meaning any person or persons acting or purporting to act for or on behalf of any faction, party, department, agency, bureau, or military force of or within a foreign country, or for or on behalf of any government or any person or persons purporting to act as a government within a foreign country, whether or not such government is recognized by the United States;

The term "communication intelligence" means all procedures and methods used in the interception of communications and the obtaining of information from such communications by other than the intended recipients;

The term "unauthorized person" means any person who, or agency which, is not authorized to receive information of the categories set forth in subsection (a) of this section, by the President, or by the head of a department or agency of the United States Government which is expressly designated by the President to engage in communication intelligence activities for the United States.

(c) Nothing in this section shall prohibit the furnishing, upon lawful demand, of information to any regularly constituted committee of the Senate or House of Representatives of the United States of America, or joint committee thereof.

U.S.C 18 - 799. Violation of regulations of National Aeronautics and Space Administration

Whoever willfully shall violate, attempt to violate, or conspire to violate any regulation or order promulgated by the Administrator of the National Aeronautics and Space Administration for the protection of security of any laboratory, station, base or other facility, or part thereof, or any aircraft, missile, spacecraft, or similar vehicle, or part thereof, or other property or equipment in the custody of any contractor under any contract with the Administration or any subcontractor of any such contractor, shall be fined not more than $15,000, or imprisoned not more than one year, or both.

U.S.C. 18 - 2153. Destruction of war material, war premises, or war utilities

(a) Whoever, when the United States is at war, or in times of national emergency as declared by the President or by the Congress, with intent to injure, interfere with, or obstruct the United States or any associate nation in preparing for or carrying on the war or defense activities, or, with reason to believe that his act may injure, interfere with, or obstruct the United States or any associate nation in preparing for or carrying on the war or defense activities, willfully injures, destroys, contaminates or infects or attempts so injure, destroy, contaminate or infect so any war material, war premises, or war utilities, shall be fined not more than $10,000 or imprisoned not more than 30 years, or both.

(b) If two or more persons conspire to violate this section, and one or more of such persons do any act to effect the object of the conspiracy, each of the parties to such conspiracy, shall be punished as provided in subsection (a) of this section.

U.S.C. 18 - 2154. Production of defective war material, war premises, or war utilities

(a) Whoever, when the United States is at war, or in times of national emergency as declared by the President or by the Congress, with intent to injure, interfere with, or obstruct the United States or any associate nation in preparing for or carrying on the war or defense activities, or, with reason to believe that his act may injure, interfere with, or obstruct the United States or any associate nation in preparing for or carrying on the war or defense activities, willfully makes, constructs, or causes to be made or constructed in a defective manner, or attempts to make, construct, or cause to be made or constructed in a defective manner any war material, war premises or war utilities, or any tool, implement, machine, utensil, or receptacle used or employed in making, producing manufacturing, or repairing any such war material, war premises or war utilities, shall be fined not more than $10,000 or imprisoned not more than 30 years, or both.

(b) If two or more persons conspire to violate this section, and one or more of such persons do any act to effect the object of the conspiracy, each of the parties to such conspiracy shall be punished as provided in subsection (a) of this section.

U.S.C. 18 - 2155. Destruction of National defense materials, national defense premises or national defense facilities

(a) Whoever, with intent to injure, interfere with, or obstruct the national defense of the United States, willfully injures, destroys, contaminates or infects, or attempts to so injure, destroy, contaminate or infect any national defense material, national defense premises, or national defense utilities, shall be fined not more than $10,000 or imprisoned not more than 10 years, or both.

(b) If two or more persons conspire to violate this section, and one or more of such persons do any act to effect the object of the conspiracy, each of the parties to such conspiracy shall be punished as provided in subsection (a) of this section.

U.S.C. 18 - 2156. Production of defective national defense material, national defense premises or national defense utilities

(a) Whoever, with intent to injure, interfere with, or obstruct the national defense of the United States, willfully makes, constructs, or attempts to make or construct in a defective manner, any national

204 Top Secret/Trade Secret

defense material, national defense premises or national defense utilities, or any tool, implement, machine, utensil, or receptacle used or employed in making, producing, manufacturing, or repairing any such national defense material, national defense premises or national defense utilities, shall be fined not more than $10,000 or imprisoned not more than 10 years, or both.

(b) If two or more persons conspire to violate this section, and one or more of such persons do any act to effect the object of the conspiracy, each of the parties to such conspiracy shall be punished as provided in subsection (a) of this section.

U.S.C. 18 - 371. Conspiracy to commit offense or to defraud United States

If two or more persons conspire either to commit any offense against the United States, or to defraud the United States, or any agency thereof in any manner or for any purpose, and one or more of such persons do any act to effect the object of the conspiracy, each shall be fined not more than $10,000 or imprisoned not more than five years, or both.

U.S.C. 50 - 797. Security regulations and orders; penalty for violation

(a) Whoever willfully shall violate any such regulation or order as, pursuant to lawful authority, shall be or has been promulgated or approved by the Secretary of Defense, or by any military commander designated by the Secretary of Defense, or by the Director of the National Advisory Committee for Aeronautics, for the protection or security of military or naval aircraft, airports, airport facilities, vessels, harbors, ports, piers, waterfront facilities, bases, forts, posts, laboratories, stations, vehicles, equipment, explosives, or other property or places subject to the jurisdiction, administration, or in the custody of the Department of Defense, any Department or agency of which said Department consists, or any officer or employee of said Department or agency, or of the National Advisory Committee for Aeronautics or any officer or employee thereof, relating to fire hazards, fire protection, lighting, machinery, guard service, disrepair, disuse or other unsatisfactory conditions thereon, or the ingress thereto or agress or removal of persons there-from, or otherwise providing for safeguarding the same against destruction, loss, or injury by accident or by enemy action, sabotage or other subversive actions, shall be guilty of a misdemeanor and upon conviction thereof shall be liable to a fine of not to exceed $5,000 or to imprisonment for not more than one year, or both.

(b) Every such regulation or order shall be posted in conspicuous and appropriate places.

NOTE: Reprinted from the Department of Defense, *Industrial Security Manual for Safeguarding Classified Information.* Washington: GPO; 1984 March; DOD 5220.22-m. 345p.

Index